MILTON
AND
THE NATURE OF MAN

BY THE SAME AUTHOR

T. S. Eliot: His Mind and Art (1962)
The First Sphere: A Study in Kierkegaardian Aesthetics (1965)
Studies in Poetry (1970)
Critics and Criticism (1971)

MILTON

AND
THE NATURE OF MAN

A DESCRIPTIVE STUDY OF *PARADISE LOST* IN TERMS OF THE
CONCEPT OF MAN AS THE IMAGE OF GOD

A. G. GEORGE

PR
3562
G4

ASIA PUBLISHING HOUSE
NEW YORK

© A. G. GEORGE, 1974
Arapara Ghevarghese **George** (1929)

All rights reserved. No part of this publication may be reproduced, stored in a retrieval system, or transmitted, in any form or by any means, electronic, mechanical, photocopying, recording or otherwise, without the prior permission of the Publisher.

ISBN 0.210.40552.X

PRINTED IN INDIA
AT ANANDA PRESS, LUCKNOW AND PUBLISHED BY P. S. JAYASINGHE, ASIA PUBLISHING HOUSE, INC., 420, LEXINGTON AVENUE, NEW YORK, 10017

To

RUPIN

PREFACE

This book is on the concept of man which emerges from Milton's works. The relevance of this concept to the criticism and interpretation of *Paradise Lost* can never be over-emphasized.

It has almost become a generally accepted assumption that the only way to formulate doctrines of human nature is to ground them in psychology of some variety or other. The validity of this assumption seems to be taken for granted, in literary criticism at least, without sufficient scrutiny. Accordingly, in Milton Criticism too, we find a persistent effort to employ Seventeenth-Century psychology to formulate Milton's doctrine of man. Can this be done fruitfully, without violating the poetic integrity of a work like *Paradise Lost* with its epic concerns? This is one of the most important questions which I have attempted to examine at some length. In the Introduction, I have outlined the character and the scope of the critical problems selected for consideration.

I have not sought to re-duplicate existing knowledge on the subject. Psychological interpretations of Milton's doctrine of man are many; likewise, there are scholarly studies on the relationship which obtains in Milton's writings, between individual and collective organisations such as the religious and socio-political institutions. I must especially mention two important works which I found very useful: *Milton in the Puritan Revolution* (1941) by Donald M. Wolfe, and *Milton and the Puritan Dilemma* (1942) by Arthur E. Barker. There are also the extremely useful and elaborate Introductions in the Yale Edition of Milton's Prose. And there are many, many more. If knowledge of all these is not explicitly shown in this book either through reviewing their contents or through citing them, it is only because these constitute the general bases on which I erect my theories. Indeed, no student of Milton Studies who advances new theories can do so except by standing on the shoulders of giants in his field.

The fact that some important names are omitted from discussion in the book does not necessarily mean that I am not aware of their works. In all discussions of recent Milton Criticism, I have been concerned not with individuals, however important, but with tendencies and movements. Thus I have taken either the earliest or the best representatives of movements in Milton Criticism, and attempted to discuss them from a historical perspective, and examine the formative conceptions which determine tendencies and movements.

Seventeenth-Century Studies have thrown much light on Milton's use of contemporary ideas in *Paradise Lost*. But there are other areas of interest in this epic and these are my concerns.

The Seventeenth-Century reader of *Paradise Lost* (I mean Milton's contemporary) may not have emerged from this epic any more successfully than the reader in any other time or clime. To Milton's contemporaries, many ideas in *Paradise Lost* may have been well known and familiar. But ideas are not poetry. Milton is not a skilled versifier, mumbling in verse Seventeenth-Century commonplaces. He is a creative poet whose intuitions capture new insights, and the vigour of whose intellect shapes original conceptions.

I am not minimizing the relevance of Milton scholarship to Milton criticism. I only wish to stress that in the controversy regarding Milton's poetical achievements, criticism and interpretation too have a significant role to play.

In quoting Milton's poetry I have used Merritt Y. Hughes's edition, *John Milton : Complete Poems and Major Prose*. For quotations from Milton's prose, I have used the Columbia edition of *The Works of John Milton*, edited by Frank Allen Patterson. The spellings have been retained as they are in these editions. The only abbreviation I have used is "PL" for *Paradise Lost*. The complete citations for the books quoted here have been given only in the Bibliography.

I should like to express my sincere thanks to Professor Edward Said of the Department of English and Comparative Literatures, Columbia University, and the other members of the faculty, for their unfailing courtesy to me which made my stay at the University both enjoyable and fruitful. To my friend and colleague, Dr. R. W. Desai of the Department of English, University of Delhi, I owe a deep debt of gratitude for his keen interest in my work which made him read through the typescript and correct and edit it with painstaking thoroughness.

A. G. G.

Columbia University
New York
January 1972

CONTENTS

Preface   *vii*

CHAPTER I   Introduction   1

CHAPTER II   Preliminary Problems and Points of View   11

CHAPTER III   Milton's Conception of the Human Soul and its Relation to the Classical and Christian Traditions   18

CHAPTER IV   Reason as an Element in Man's Divine Image and Likeness   30

CHAPTER V   Other Dimensions of Human Nature, and the Reformation Contribution to the Doctrine of Man   42

CHAPTER VI   The Dignity of Man   54

CHAPTER VII   The Top of Speculation: Man Embraces Woman   65

CHAPTER VIII   Was Adam "Fallen" before He Fell?   75

CHAPTER IX   A Literary Theory of Myth and History   90

CHAPTER X   The "Genesis" Myths and History. Arnold J. Toynbee on the Genesis Myths   101

CHAPTER XI   Structure and Theme in *Paradise Lost*   114

CHAPTER XII   Crisis and Resolution in *Paradise Lost*: Man as Free and as Fallen   136

Bibliography   159

Index   165

MILTON
AND
THE NATURE OF MAN

CHAPTER ONE

INTRODUCTION

To EVERY INGENIOUS way of attacking Milton there corresponds an equally ingenious way of defending him. Sir Walter Raleigh's heavy broadsides against *Paradise Lost* in the beginning of our century sent many Miltonists for shelter to the thick jungle of Seventeenth-Century Studies. They took their Milton too with them for protection. But he is too big even for its tropical luxuriance, and he stands out dwarfing everything around him. Another set of pro-Miltonists clambered up the knees of that giant from Greece, Plato. Safely seated on his shoulders, they Platonize Milton. "Not from Genesis, but from Greece," they cry, "comes the philosophy of Milton." And Milton is defended!

My book has no part to play in this Titanomachy. Its modest aim is to explore a less noisy and less crowded field. Like the Satan of Milton's *Paradise Lost*, its strategy is directed towards "some new Race call'd Man, about this time/To be created like to us, though less/In Power and excellence" (II. 348-350). And like this Satan again, we will try to seduce this new "race of upstart Creatures" called Man, and with his assistance try and make some inroads into *Paradise Lost*, especially into Books Four, Five, Eight, Nine, and Ten.

In other words, what conceptions about human nature emerge from Milton's prose and poetry? And what ideas about human reality are most relevant to the reading of *Paradise Lost* in order to establish those links among the epic incidents in the poem, which monistic preconceptions, Platonic or Puritan, about Milton's philosophy, ethics, psychology, and narrative, do not provide? Thus Milton's doctrine of human nature is our field of enquiry. Many aspects of this problem have received scholarly attention, but many more remain to be examined.

In studying the problems of characterization with reference to Adam and Eve, and the general philosophy of ethics in Milton's poem, scholars from the time of Edwin Greenlaw and James Holly Hanford onwards have assumed with a show of reason that *Paradise Lost* is essentially a Platonic poem, and that Milton's philosophy of life on the whole is Platonic.

The thesis advanced in Edwin Greenlaw's paper "A Better Teacher than Aquinas" is famous.[1] Arguing on the assumption that "Milton was the poetical son of Spenser," and further on the basis of Spenser's Platonism, Greenlaw concluded that *Paradise Lost* not less than the *Faerie Queene* is a "moral allegory," and not poetical theology, and that "what justifies God's dealings with men, Milton's theme in *Paradise Lost*, is that God tests through trial the virtues of temperance, justice, and continence".[2]

Furthermore, "Obedience then is not blind but a matter of choice and this choice involves abstaining through temperance, the rational principle of the soul, or yielding through excess, the irrational principle".[3]

In short, Greenlaw has tried to establish that the philosophic content of *Paradise Lost* is a kind of Platonic Idealism which teaches through the doctrine of temperance. In his view, the story of the fall immediately "gains significance and interest if we recognize that the apple is but a symbol, and that Milton's real theme is to show how Adam fell because he did not stand the test of temperance".[4]

These arguments themselves would not have interested us, had it not been for the fact that they find extended application in more sustained studies on *Paradise Lost*. Moreover, these very arguments lend themselves conveniently into the hands of anti-Milton critics. Quite evidently, Greenlaw is wrong in that he tacitly equates the contents of Plato's philosophy with the simple ethical idealism of the Temperance doctrine. Nothing is said about the poetic implications of Plato's philosophical anthropology, or of his metaphysics, both of which are equally relevant to Milton's poetry. Greenlaw identifies the substance of Milton's theory of human nature with the substance of his ethical teachings. At any rate, the essence of ethical puritanism remains, the only change being that the old Biblical puritanism has been replaced with Platonic puritanism.

It is here that my points of departure emerge. While Platonism is certainly an important component of Milton's philosophy of life, we notice also everywhere in Milton the persistence of the Biblical

---

[1] *Studies in Philology*, xiv (1917), 196-217.
[2] *Ibid.*, p. 200.
[3] *Ibid.*, pp. 200-1.
[4] *Ibid.*, p. 213.

view of the nature of man. There is an element of truth in Wordsworth's observation (in the "Preface" To *Poems*, 1815) that "however imbued the surface might be with classical literature, he [Milton] was a Hebrew in soul; and all things tended in him towards the sublime."

These Hebrew and Biblical elements seem to have determined the essential nature of Milton's view of human reality.

There is a fundamental difference between Plato's theory of human nature and Milton's. This difference relates to the respective doctrines on the very origin of man. True, in Plato and in Milton (as also in the Bible) anthropology precedes psychology, and it is also true that their anthropologies are essentially theo-centric. But there the similarity ends. Here also begins the wide cleavage between Platonic anthropology and the Christian anthropology which is Milton's.

In Plato's theo-centric anthropology, the origin of mankind is in the alienation of the soul from its True and Eternal Abode. This alienation, in so far as it accounts for the origin of man, corresponds to the Biblical idea of the creation of man. But in Plato's thought this alienation itself is evil, and the origin of man too is evil. But in Milton's thought (as in the Bible), man's origin lies in Divine Forethought, and Divine Creation. And having been created by God, after deliberative decision and through the principle of love, all created beings are good. The origin of man is good; nay, very good. "And God saw everything that he had made, and, behold, it was very good" (Genesis, 1.31).

In Biblical thought (as in Milton's), evil is accidental; it came through sin. It came into the world through a voluntary and specific act of man, and it lies in man's power to overcome it. The idea of sin or evil is not intrinsic to the Christian-Miltonic definition of man. In Plato it is the root-conception and the principal term in defining man, as a being alienated from God and from His True and Eternal Heaven of Ideas. Simply stated, in the Bible the origin of man is viewed as good; in Plato, as evil. Here lies the radically irreconcilable point of departure between the Platonic tradition and the Christian-Miltonic tradition in philosophical anthropology. St. Augustine learnt to his cost in the end that the circle of Platonism cannot be squared against the Christian faith.

Speaking with special reference to *Paradise Lost*, we come up against many facts which Platonism will not be able to stomach. For instance, Plato would not have been able to look on with innocent amusement and approval, as Milton in his role as the epic poet does, on Adam's pre-lapsarian sexual intercourse in Eden (IV, 740ff). Nor will Plato's angels do what Raphael tells Adam that they do, as a matter of course, in Heaven, though he (Raphael) blushes "Celestial rosy red, Love's proper hue" (VIII, 619). There are other instances besides these. In short, the spirit of Milton's in doctrinal content in *Paradise Lost* points in the direction of the the validating of the flesh, regardless of whether the flesh indulges in excesses, or behaves strictly according to the Doctrine of Mean.

Tangentially related to Greenlaw's position is that of James Holly Hanford. In an article entitled "The Dramatic Element in *Paradise Lost*" (in the same 1917-Issue of *Studies in Philology*), he maintains that "psychology and analyses are his [Milton's] aim in so far as the merely human aspect of the story [of *Paradise Lost*] is concerned."[5]

Hanford's purpose is to establish the dramatic quality of the plot and the epic action in *Paradise Lost*. He does this by a careful comparison of the similarities in theme, situation, and tragic sentiment in Milton and in the Elizabethan Tragedy. Hanford is eager to refute the charge that Milton is a mere epic poet, living in the mythic world of abstractions, and having no knowledge of the realities of human nature. And he is thus led to postulate the relation between "character and destiny", in Adam's fall. In *Paradise Lost*, says he, Out of the puzzle of character and destiny springs a sympathy for struggling, taxed humanity which no theologian can give.[6]

But if the general principle that character is destiny holds in *Paradise Lost* and if Adam's character is his destiny, then the ground has been prepared for the most effective, and one of the most powerful, attacks on Milton, that of A.J.A. Waldock.

In this Introduction I have thus adopted the unusual procedure of outlining the theses against which my book has attempted to provide the antitheses. Against these positions, I argue that in Milton's theory of the nature of man, the most important element is his doctrine of the origin of man; that Milton's anthropology is theological and Biblical, and not Platonic; that this can be proved

[5] *Ibid.*, p. 183.
[6] *Ibid.*, p. 194.

on the basis of Milton's prose and the two epic poems. Accordingly, the basic assumption in Milton is that man has been created in God's image and likeness. In his thought and art, there is no understanding of man apart from the meaning of this phrase, "God's image and likeness." Even Milton's psychology is derived from this. And here I mean by "psychology" the doctrine of the subjective consciousness, or the doctrine of the subjective spirit of man. Faculty Psychology of "reason-versus-passions" is only part of the auxiliary equipment in *Paradise Lost*. It is not its central doctrine of man.

Christian philosophy of man from the earliest century to our own, from the time of St. Irenaeus (born *circa* A.D. 130) to that of Karl Barth, centres around the absolutely axiomatic belief that man has been created in the image and likeness of God. This is the first element in all revealed faith. It has always remained the cornerstone of Christian thought. It is so in Milton too. Witness the number of times such phrases as "God's image in man", "man's divine similitude," and similar ones, occur and recur in the prose and poetry of Milton. In *Paradise Lost*, their recurrence is too frequent to be pointed out.

Now this concept of man as God's image and likeness developed by incremental addition from philosopher to philosopher, from theologian to theologian. The history of this doctrine is the history of Christian theology. From St. Irenaeus up to the time of St. Augustine and St. Aquinas it meant the "rationality" of man, rationality defined, as Milton does, as man's capacity to know and to love God. With the Reformation, and with Luther and Calvin, the concept acquired further extensions of meanings. Luther stressed two meanings in particular, man's rule over, and overlordship of, the rest of the creation (along with other ideas relating to man's supremacy over all nature), and also the idea of man's original righteousness.

Calvin extended its conceptual implications further, emphasizing the glory of man in the scale of creation, and the idea of the dignity of man. Strangely enough, many people do not realise that the Christian conception of human dignity and glory is essentially Calvin's contribution.

Milton telescoped all these conceptions into a complex image, and for descriptive effects, exploited to the full their poetic potentialities in presenting Adam, Eve, the Garden of Eden, and the crisis of the fall. If we read Books Three, Four, Five, Seven, and Eight of this epic, bearing in mind the imagistic and the conceptual implications of the phrase "man's divine image and likeness," our reading will be enriched through a deeper understanding of the connections between descriptions, episodes, dialogues, and soliloquies. I am not saying that Milton borrowed each of these conceptions separately from each theologian, and reworked them into his poetry. On the contrary, these are among the universal constants in Christian thought, and without having to borrow them especially for the composition of *Paradise Lost*, they already constituted the stock of Christian ideas in Milton's mind. Indeed no Christian who is seriously interested in the intellectual implications of his faith in any century or period can be ignorant of the doctrine that man was made in the image of God and in His likeness, and the theological elaborations of its meanings.

Passing beyond these, I have touched on Milton's own original extension of the meaning of "God's image" in man. It will become quite clear that Milton included in his theory of the nature of man the idea of humanity also. This idea involves the conception of an ideal human relationship, exemplified at its best in the pre-lapsarian relationship of conjugal love in Adam and Eve. Neither in Christian philosophy nor in Milton's thought can we find the idea of individuality without its inseparable correlate of humanity. The idea of man's individuality is inseparable from its conceptual correlates the ideas of humanity and of human relationship. This may appear somewhat inconsistent with Milton's rugged individualism. But it is not so, for in Milton the idea of relationship, especially conjugal relationship, is central to his conception of human nature. To him, conjugal love at its best is the culmination of one's love for the other person, the supreme illustration of love for one's neighbour, than which there is nothing greater. The sexual factor in marital love is subordinated to the ontological possibility of being united with another being. Christian anthropology on the whole does not stress so much the individuality of man as much as his humanity. Modern theologians have developed this conception in detail, independently of Milton. One can mention Karl Barth's theories of human nature in his *Church Dogmatics*, which clearly set forth the Christian idea of humanity. When God created man, "male and female created He them." The sexual differentiation, while it establishes a separateness, also emphasizes the possibility of a union through this very differentiation. And the two shall be one flesh. By analogous argument the principle of oneness in manyness through the power of neighbourly love is extended to the whole of humanity. The solidarity of a united brotherhood between man and man, and the communion of fellowship are essential ingredients in the meaning of God's image in man. Milton weaves these varying shades of ideas into the texture of his *Paradise Lost*.

At the time when Milton wrote the epic, there were no theological parallels or antecedents for these doctrinal developments. His own poetic imagination created them. In doing so, that he was right within the limits of theological propriety is shown by similar developments in thought in our time. I have here referred to Karl Barth. For a study in the analogous developments in Christian thought, I have compared passages from the Divorce Pamphlets and *Paradise Lost*, with Barth's *Church Dogmatics*. I do not wish to minimize the importance of the Platonic and philosophic dimensions of *Paradise Lost*. I want only to stress the relevance of its theological framework to the task of critical interpretation.

Poetry is neither philosophy nor theology. Poetry is not poetization of a content. It is an integral mode of experience, as valid as the other two. Theological belief may enrich poetry through its own mythical framework and the conceptual contents comprehended within it.

Directly connected with the mythology of *Paradise Lost* are the problems of narrative, and the technique of its plot-construction. To what extent has Milton succeeded in artistically transforming the simple Bible story of the creation of man and his fall? There are two possible answers to this question. One is that Milton did not succeed in correlating the incidents of the narrative into a closely-knit plot. And the epic plot is always discussed in comparison with the plots in drama. Thus this school of criticism—an early example of which is Hanford's "Dramatic Elements in *Paradise Lost*," referred to earlier—seeks to discover the relation between character and destiny in the poem, and the presence of adequate characterological motivations in Adam and Eve. According to this school of critics, if Milton has succeeded in constructing an epic plot in the poem, then the crisis of the poem, that is, the fall of man, must necessarily follow, and be causally connected with the traits, impulses, and the other psychological qualities delineated in the characters of Adam and Eve. Most Milton

Studies in our time, besides Stylistic Criticism, and Seventeenth-Century Studies, are variations on this basic theme. The pro-Miltonists of our century, from Hanford to Douglas Bush and Northrop Frye, defend *Paradise Lost* arguing that the characterological motivation in *Paradise Lost* is adequate, and that the fall of Adam and Eve follows logically from the qualities latent in them. (I have reviewed some of these theories in Chapter Eight.)

But here comes the rub. On logically extending the principle of motivation to all the relevant causes in the poem, we find that not only do the bad impulses in Adam and Eve create the antecedent conditions of the fall, but also that such noble sentiments like love are equally responsible for it. This latter position constitutes the main plank from which one adverse school of criticism is launched against Milton.

This too is the central thesis of A. J. A. Waldock in his *"Paradise Lost" and its Critics* (1947). "Adam falls through love," he insists. This, as he argues further, is absurd, for love is man's noblest emotion, and if in Milton's epic, love leads to the fall of man, then there is something wrong with either Milton the poet as the maker of his plot, or the mythology on which he based his epic. According to Waldock both criticisms hold. He says that Milton lacked that enrichment of experience which comes by handling human emotions realistically as is done through the technique of the novel. In modern times we have acquired this experience. But "poor" Milton was without it. So then, as Hanford compared *Paradise Lost* with the drama, Waldock compares it with the modern novel. F.R. Leavis once called Waldock's *"Paradise Lost" and its Critics* one of the best books so far on Milton. True, Waldock provides all the right answers to the wrong questions. And the absurdity of some of his conclusions is the absurdity of a *reductio ad absurdum*.

I have in every chapter tried to indicate my differences with Waldock, taking him as a typical and standard representative of those critics who highlighted the problems of narrative techniques in *Paradise Lost*. His views have been ably challenged from several quarters, and many recent attempts have been made to prove that *Paradise Lost* is a logical epic. Attempts have also been made to interpret the metaphorical and the mythical structures in it.

I have developed a theory of the myth, and tested its applicability to Milton's epic. In this theory, the psychoanalytical and the anthropological elements have been excluded. "Myth" is used here in a strictly literary sense, emphasizing the relation between the narrative structure in a verbal composition and the view of reality which this structure comprehends. Viewed in this sense, the "myth" is a narrative in which reality is conceived as a structure, and not as a process. The plot, on the other hand, is a narrative structure which presents reality as a process. In other words, in any literary composition in which the underlying theory of reality is structural (as contra-distinguished from the causal), we have a mythic narrative.

The processive theory of reality with its principle of causality, and the structural theory of reality with its corresponding principle of "relation" are the two great systematizations of human experiences on the whole. In the sphere of creative literature, both theories, the processive and the structural, are relevant. Any creative composition which stresses process and causality organizes itself as a plot; and any composition, in prose or verse, which emphasizes structure and relation shapes itself into a literary "myth."

It is in this sense that the concept of the myth has been applied to *Paradise Lost*. I have not, however, altogether eliminated the principle of logical connection in the narrative, or the principle of cause in characterizations, from my discussions of the epic. But I have subsumed them under the conception of structural relationships in the myth of the narrative.

The problem of problems in Milton Criticism is that of Milton's technique of handling the fall of man in the poem. The art by which he transforms the simple Bible story of the fall into the complex crisis of an epic action appears to defy analysis and elucidation. To say that this transformation has not been achieved is simply to resign ourselves to critical escapism. As in the Bible, so in Milton, the fall story has to be explained. But all explanations can go only up to a point, beyond which, as Kierkegaard says, the explanation itself has to be explained.

With the fall came sin into the world. The fall did not come through sin. Here is that critical and philosophical paradox which all explanations seek to explain away. All interpretative criticisms of *Paradise Lost* too must come to grips with this paradox, without straining and stretching it logically. As Kierkegaard says, "To want to explain logically the entrance of sin into the world is a stupidity which could only occur to people who are comically anxious to get an explanation.'"[7]

It is quite comical to see so many critics of *Paradise Lost* continuing to struggle with the principle of causality in order to explain and defend the structure of its plot. This principle still casts its spell on the critical intellect when philosophical thought on the whole, including the philosophy of science itself, has overthrown it long ago.

I have compared Milton's treatment of the fall of man with Kierkegaard's treatment of it in *The Concept of Dread*, without forcing any conclusions.

The myth is related to reality through its symbolic content. We should also examine its relation to history, for the "myth" or "mythology" is not simple "pre-history." One of our leading philosophers of history in the Modern Age, Arnold J. Toynbee, has developed a theory of history in which mythologies provide analogues for historical processes. He has chosen, in particular, the "genesis myth" which deals with the origin of mankind in one story or the other. These myths embody and illustrate the operation of the basic dynamisms in the historical destiny of mankind. I have used Toynbee's analysis of the genesis myths of "Superhuman conflicts" to see if some structural problems in Milton's epic could be elucidated.

This Introduction is rather long because, in view of the unusual character of my concerns in the book, I wanted to explain the nature and scope of my problems, and indicate the methods of my approach. It has touched upon the main foci of interest in the book. I may here mention that I have not concerned myself with the problems of epic style in Milton Criticism. Criticisms of Milton's style, initiated by T. S. Eliot and vigorously followed up by F.R. Leavis and others, do not alone constitute the hub of modern Milton controversy.

[7] *The Concept of Dread*, p. 45.

CHAPTER TWO

PRELIMINARY PROBLEMS AND POINTS OF VIEW

THE COMPLEXITY OF Milton's thought and the variety of approaches to it compel critics to adopt definite points of view on all important critical issues. Initially the points of departure may not differ conspicuously and substantially, but their logical pursuits will in the end lead to widely diverging perspectives on Milton's art and thought. Milton has left behind him a considerable body of prose writings which expound views and convictions on almost every important aspect of life. To assess the relevance of these attitudes and convictions in the context of those obtained from his poetry is one important problem.

It is possible to read the prose as a gloss on the poetry of Milton, as Maurice Kelley does in his comparison of Milton's treatise on the Christian Doctrine with *Paradise Lost*. But the validity of this procedure has been questioned by others. They argue that it is dangerous to the integrity of Milton's poems to regard his prose as their deliberate annotations. There are yet other critics who treat the prose works themselves as formal compositions, as the poems are, and stress the considerations of form to the exclusion of the idea content in the study of prose. And they warn us against treating ideas in prose as beliefs. This is another problem which demands either a solution, or, at least, a point of view. According to Kester Svendsen (in *Milton and Science*) the formality with which Milton addresses himself to his subject should warn us not to identify the worldview there with Milton's own worldview. Neither should we, in his view, attempt to establish from the prose the attitudes in the poems written at the same time. This is a strange assumption.

A third problem is the relation between Milton's intellectual milieu, and the development of his own thought. This has been closely investigated by scholars of eminence. It has provoked a considerable amount of "source studies" of Milton's mind, and of the origins and sources of the ideas in *Paradise Lost*. If Milton is only reflecting borrowed ideas, then his poetry is a monument to a dead intellectual world. The modernity of Milton's thought has been denied, on this assumption. Sir Walter Raleigh dismissed *Paradise Lost* with the remark, "The *Paradise Lost* is not the less an eternal monument because it is a monument to dead ideas" (*Milton*, p. 85). (Contemporary echoes of Raleigh's comments are heard in our time.) He was commenting on Mark Pattison's complaint that Milton had mistaken a scheme of life for life itself, and for that reason, it required a violent effort from the reader of modern times to accommodate his concepts to the anthropocentric theology of the poem.

Pattison has unwittingly expressed a significant truth, although he has not probably grasped its significance. It is a fact that life can be apprehended only as a "scheme of life." All understanding of life is a schematization of experience. Milton did create a scheme of life in his poetry, and that is one of its main merits. We further maintain that this scheme comprehended a far wider range of phenomena than was ever taken for the theme of a single poem. In another sense too Pattison's stricture implies praise. To have created a scheme of life is to have created a worldview which is far from being a simple reflection of contemporary life.

My own position in respect of these problems can be briefly, though not dogmatically, stated here. I believe that with Milton's metaphysical commitments, artistic creation would not be conceivable without a central nucleus of ideas. His poetry and prose thus comprehend a scheme of life and thought. Its "modernity" has to be assessed in relation to its permanent significance.

Literary criticism cannot ignore the recurrence of ideas and motifs in prose and poetry. When similar or identical motifs of themes and ideas recur in different media of writing, they illustrate the author's system of beliefs and attitudes. Thus Milton's prose is neither to be considered as formal compositions, nor as systematic commentary on the poetry. But his poetry and prose together reveal his mind and also his formal concerns.

The formal concerns of an author reveal not only his artistic conscience, but also the quality of his commitments to life. The moral earnestness of purpose shows itself through the rigour of formal discipline. In the case of a poetic imagination like Milton's which is characterized not by "negative capability" but—to use Professor Ellmann's phrase for Yeat's view of the poetic imagination—by "affirmative capability," the more serious the commitment to art, the greater will the commitment to life be.

I have already referred to a recent criticism which denies Milton any interest in, or knowledge of, life. This criticism attempts to carry conviction by comparing the mythological background of *Paradise Lost* with the realism of the novel. The mythology of the epic, it is said, does not demand from the poet a thorough knowledge of human nature. Reference has also been made to A. J. A. Waldock who developed this theory in detail. We have to examine here his assumptions more closely. He says:

> We have acquired, in plain fact—through the novel and in other ways—certain types of literary experience that Milton was without. It is not absurd to mention the novel in connection with *Paradise Lost*, for the characteristic problems of such a poem and the characteristic problems of the novel have elements in common. The novel has given us an enormous store of precedents. Largely as a result of its history we have built up a technique for assessing at once the practicability of certain themes for literary treatment, a technique that...Milton did not possess in quite the same sense.[1]

He continues to argue that the fable of *Paradise Lost* has the gravest flaws, and that these flaws are reflected in Milton's handling of it.

The absurdity of this comparison between an epic and a novel has already been pointed out from several quarters. In order to read an epic as though it were a novel, we have to introduce a kind of "moral naturalism," or, the simple naturalistic ethics which has no place in an epic. But this is precisely what many critics do while they seek to establish the presence of adequate motivation for the crisis of the fall in *Paradise Lost*. Waldock has only made this absurdity more explicit by logically extending it. Commenting on Waldock, Bernard Bergonzi says:

> If one found this statement in an undergraduate essay one might scribble a question mark in the margin and ask for some evidence. The assumption is absolutely central to Waldock's approach: it seems to me far from self-evident, but he gives no reasons for making it. Waldock uses it to deduce a monistic

[1] *"Paradise Lost" and its Critics*, p. 18.

conception of 'narrative' which can apply equally to the epic and the realistic novel, and which is, in fact, so attenuated as to be entirely useless.... The fact is that modern fiction deals, for the most part, with men, and in their fallen state, rather than supernatural or pre-lapsarian beings. Behaviour in the novel is inevitably involved with a complex of assumptions relating to an existing order of society, and the conventions governing the form are intensely naturalistic.[2]

Some important problems in relation to the epic art of handling its human material emerge for consideration here. The epic poet views man mainly as an ethical being, not only in relation to other human beings, but more importantly in terms of his ultimate answerability to a trans-human dimension of values. In the epic characterization the most important considerations are the ideal possibilities of human nature. What human nature ought to be is the central question. The idea of the epic conflict derives from this conception. The epic conflict invariably is the product of the tension between its characters' ability and adequacy of endowments to perform some task, however heroic, or conform to some pattern of life and conduct however noble and exacting, and the insurmountability of the obstacles they have to face in the process of accomplishment or of fulfilment. Moral self-consciousness and an awareness of involvement in large shaping forces of human destiny or human history expressing themselves in heroic decisions or actions distinguish the general qualities of the epic hero.

The novel on the other hand provides scope for the analytical penetration of the interior of its characters: their psychology, the analysis of their impulses at the very source itself, the motivations of their actions and reactions to any given social context define, in general, the important elements in fictional characterization. Psychological realism is an indispensable requirement in the novel. The novelist should dissect and display the inner impulses and the interior forebodings of his characters and trace their expression in action.

E.M.W. Tillyard, in *The English Epic and its Background*, discusses the differences in the treatment of the theme of human nature in the novel and in the epic. Ultimately, it is human nature which is

[2] "Criticism and the Milton Controversy" in *The Living Milton*. Essays by Various Hands. Collected and edited by Frank Kermode, pp. 177ff.

the larger theme of both. But the differences in the forms determine the respective treatments at the same theme. In Tillyard's view, thus, the art of characterization in the novel, as in the epic, is controlled by its form. In the epic, characterization should give the impression of deliberateness, the presence of a notable exercise of will in the conduct of the hero or in the poet's own accomplishment.³ This is quite different from the total impression created by the novel.

The techniques of narrative and plot construction too differ accordingly. The epic theme treats of a universal human experience; but not so the novel. The epic theme assumes the aspect of universality, and accordingly, it acquires a symbolic content. Therefore the epic cannot be governed by principles of narrative realism, or of psychological probability, or of logical and causal processiveness in the correlation of the incidents, as the novel is.

As I have said earlier, the epic fable tends to assume the pattern of the "myth," in the sense that its incidents are related by symbolic connections. Commenting on the epic myth in Virgil, C.S. Lewis writes:

> ...so true an artist as Virgil could not be content with the clumsiness and monotony of a mere chronicle. His solution of the problem—one of the most important revolutions in the history of poetry—was to take one single national legend and treat it in such a way that we feel the vaster theme to be somehow implicit in it. He has to tell a comparatively shorter story and give us the illusion of having lived through a great space of time. He has to deal with a number of personages and make us feel as if national, or almost cosmic, issues are involved. He must locate his action in a legendary past and yet make us feel the present, and the intervening centuries already foreshadowed. After Virgil and Milton, this procedure seems obvious enough. But it is only because a great poet, faced with an all but insoluble problem, discovered this answer and with it discovered new possibilities for poetry itself.⁴

Without imparting some symbolic significance, no fable can be transformed into an epic narrative. Virgil, according to C. S.

³ *The English Epic and its Background*, p. 11.
⁴ *A Preface to Paradise Lost*, p. 34.

Lewis, in making his one legend "symbolical of the destiny of Rome... symbolized the destiny of Man."[5] The narrative of the epic has to incorporate, this structural quality and its symbolic meaning.

Tillyard's *The English Epic and its Background* formulates some general conceptions about the nature of epic poetry. These conceptions to some extent enable us to understand why some people find it difficult to respond to a poem like *Paradise Lost*. The substance of Tillyard's theory is as follows: in the epic there must be a fortuitous concatenation of incidents, high quality, and high seriousness, amplitude, breadth, inclusiveness, the impression of deliberate control of his material by the poet, and of his conduct in the epic hero, and an accepted unconscious metaphysics. The exuberance of material must be controlled by a powerful predetermination of it. This insistence on rigorous control and predetermination as an important element in a certain type of poetry is alien to two powerful trends in modern thought.

One is the hostility to the long poem in general. The other trend is psychological, the tendency towards valuing the spontaneous, the unconscious elements in art or in life, and towards distrusting the exercise of the conscious will, or of a controlling moral purpose. Thus Tillyard explains the awkwardness of some of our modern critics in the presence of an epic poem like *Paradise Lost*. Characterization too in the epic, instead of being "realistic," must embody the epic's symbolic meanings. To quote a relevant passage from Tillyard:

> While at home in large areas of life, the epic writer must be centred in the normal, he must measure the crooked by the straight, he must exemplify that sanity which has been claimed for true genius. No pronounced homosexual, for instance, could succeed in the epic, not so much for being one as for what his being one cuts him off from. Granted the fundamental sanity, the wider the epic poet's mental span, the better. And ideally he should be able to range from the simple sensualities to a true susceptibility to the numinous.[6]

[5] The mythic structure of *Paradise Lost,* and its symbolic significance have been discussed by Isable Gamble MacCffrey in her *Paradise Lost as "Myth"* (1959), and by Jackson I. Cope in his *The Metaphoric Structure of Paradise Lost* (1962).
[6] *The English Epic and its Background*, p. 10.

The epic presents a wider range of emotions than any other literary form, ranging from the simple sensualities to the numinous. Both character and plot must embody this range. It is in the execution of this artistic requirement that the poet's theory of the nature of man becomes determinative. To understand, respond, and evaluate the human relevance of *Paradise Lost*, we must first grasp the contents of the doctrine of human nature which is determinative to it. And, as Dr. Johnson did, if we dismiss the human interest of Milton's epic, we violate its poetic integrity.

CHAPTER THREE

MILTON'S CONCEPTION OF THE HUMAN SOUL AND ITS RELATION TO THE CLASSICAL AND CHRISTIAN TRADITIONS

IT IS IMPOSSIBLE to form a coherent doctrine of man which does not rest upon pre-suppositions, for man is too complex a phenomenon to be understood as a totality unless some principle of his nature is singled out as fundamental and used as a key principle of interpretation. This single key principle is the nature of the human soul. In Milton it is so fundamental that it governs throughout his approach to human experiences which form the themes of his poetry. For instance, one of the operative conceptions is his sense of man's dignity; another is the consciousness of temptation as the focus of moral life. Both of these can be explained in relation to his idea of the soul of man.

The mingling of religious motifs in Milton makes the exploration of any single idea in his poetry a very difficult task. It is only a commonplace to say that the two powerful conceptions which influence Milton are the Classical and the Christian. A conventional theory argues that Milton synthesized them. But when the notion of a synthesis is applied to any particular poem, it breaks down into incoherencies. Consequently we have to revise our view of Milton's synthesis, or revise our judgment of Milton as poet. And both alternatives only present the same problems, without taking us any nearer to a solution.

The influence of Plato on Milton is a case in point. That Plato, along with the Bible, is one of the two most powerful influences on Milton, no one can, and will, deny. Nevertheless when it comes to the consistent application of Platonism to any significant theme, we have to shift our ground more than once, or indulge in qualifying our statements so that the "qualifications" negate the very statements themselves.

For instance, Irene Samuel in her excellent study of the influence of Plato in Milton shows her awareness of this problem. She discusses Milton's use of the Platonic idea of the human soul, and tries to show that Milton had earlier held the same view as Plato on the human soul, and that later he abandoned it.

Apparently even after he had discarded the belief that the body and the soul are separate entities, he could make dramatic use of it. At any rate, he never completely rejected the teaching of Plato on the relative worth of body and soul.[1]

It would be an interesting problem to examine whether, on so important an issue as the nature of the soul, Milton was able to make up his mind, or not. The significance of any experience comprehended within a poem lies in its consistent interpretation from any given point of view, even if that point of view can be seriously challenged. And if Milton had not made up his mind on the question of the soul of man, and had used conceptions of the human soul in poetry without acquiring clear conceptions of it, then the treatment of his themes could not possibly be intelligent and responsible.

The truth is that Milton had made up his mind, and that in favour of the Biblical view of the human soul, although the persistent use of poetic motifs and images from classical and Platonic sources obscures the continuity of the Biblical perspectives on man and the human soul, in the writings of Milton. In a later chapter we shall show that the Biblical attitude persists as a central theme in the most Platonic of Milton's poems.

In order to clarify the problem we have to re-state some of the fundamentals of the Platonic and Biblical views on the soul, and in doing so we may only be pointing out the obvious. But sometimes even this is necessary.

In the Greek theory of the soul, of which Plato is the systematic philosopher, the soul is the mental principle considered as a substance separate from the body. Thus this theory postulates the substantial reality of the human soul. The soul is an existing entity, independent of the body, of which the individual mental life and its developments are manifestations. The individual human being is compounded of two separate realities, the soul and the body; and the life process is the uneasy equilibrium of interaction between the soul and the body. In this combination the soul is the permanent and the most important element. The body is only a temporary encasement or the prison-house for the ethereal and

[1] *Plato and Milton*, p. 158.

eternal soul. The main elements of his doctrine of the soul came from Pindar and the Orphic sources.[2] According to J.A. Stewart :

> The Soul is represented in the three Eschatological Myths of *Phaedo*, *Gorgias*, and the *Republic*, and in other myths not strictly Eschatological, as a Person created by God, and responsible to him for acts in which it is a free agent within limits set by Necessity—responsible to God throughout an existence which began before its incarnation in this body, and will continue for ever after the death of his body—an existence in which it is subject to periodical re-incarnations, alternating with terms of disembodiment, during which it receives recompense for the deeds done in the flesh; till at last—if it is not incorrigible—it is thoroughly purified by penance, and enters into the peace of a never-ending disembodied state, like that which it enjoyed in its own peculiar star, before it began the cycle of incarnations.[3]

Briefly, in the Platonic doctrine of the human soul, we have preexistence, recollection, retribution, reincarnation, final purification, and a never-ending disembodied existence of the purified soul. The dualism between the soul and body, flesh and spirit, and earth and heaven is stressed. The *Phaedo*, a powerful source of influence on early Christendom, poses very sharply the contrast between the body and the soul, and presents the opposition between them.

> For the body is a source of countless distractions by reason of the mere requirement of food, and is liable also to diseases which overtake and impede us in the pursuit of truth: it fills us full of loves, and lusts, and fears, and fancies of all kinds, and endless foolery, and in very truth, as men say, takes away from us the power of thinking at all. Whence come wars, and fightings, and factions ? Whence but from the body and the lusts of the body ? All wars are occasioned by the love of money, and money has to be acquired for the sake of the body and in slavish ministration to it.... It has been proved to us by experience that if we would have pure knowledge of anything we must be quit of the body—the soul by herself must behold things by themselves :

---

[2] See "The Socratic Doctrine of the Human Soul" by John Burnett, p. 25.
[3] *The Myths of Plato*, pp. 85-6.

and then we shall attain that which we desire, and of which we say that we are lovers—wisdom; not while we live, but, as the argument shows, only after death; for if while in company with the body the soul cannot have pure knowledge, one of two things follows—either knowledge is not to be attained at all, or, if at all, after death.... In the present life, we think that we make the nearest approach to knowledge when we have the least possible intercourse or communion with the body, and do not suffer the contagion of the bodily nature, but keep ourselves pure until the hour when God himself is pleased to release us. And thus getting rid of the foolishness of the body we may expect to be pure and hold converse with the pure, and to know with the pure, and to know of ourselves all that exists, which I take it is no other than the truth.[4]

The contrast between the body and the soul is nowhere more sharply focussed in Plato's thought than here. The soul is of the realm of Forms, the corruptible body of the realm of the Sensibles. The moral choice between them should be obvious to any rational man. This is not at all the relation between the body and the soul in Milton's theory.

Plato's psychology of the soul, explained in the *Republic*, is also of interest to us.[5] In his tripartite division of the soul, reason is the forbidding principle; the appetites urge the gratification of pleasure; and the spirit is the assertive and dynamic element making for leadership and achievement. The spirit while distinct from reason and appetite is the agent of reason, transmitting the verdict of reason to the appetite, and making it effective by the use of force upon appetite. To quote Plato:

Then we may infer that they are two, and that they differ from one another; one of them may be called the rational principle of the soul, the other, which accompanies certain pleasures and satisfaction, is that which a man loves and hungers and thirsts and feels the emotions of desire, and may be rightly termed irrational or appetitive.... Then let those be marked out as the two principles which there are existing in the soul. And what shall we say of passion, or spirit? Is that

[4] *Phaedo*, 66-7.
[5] *The Republic*, 439, 440, 441.

a third, or akin to one of the preceding ?⁶

The spirit is akin to desire, but "in the conflict of the soul, spirit is arrayed on the side of the rational principle."⁷

In the *Phaedrus* this psychology is expressed in the form of a myth.

> Let the soul be compared to a pair of winged horses and charioteer joined in natural union. Now the horses and the charioteers of the gods are all of them noble and of noble descent, but those of other races are mixed. First, you must know that the human charioteer drives a pair; and next, that one of his horses is noble and the other is ignoble...so that the management of the human chariot cannot but be a difficult and anxious task. I will endeavour to explain to you in what way the mortal differs from the immortal creature. The soul in her totality has the care of inanimate being everywhere, and traverses the whole heaven in divers forms appearing; when perfect and fully winged she soars upward, and orders the whole world; whereas the imperfect soul, losing her wings and drooping in her flight at last settles on the solid ground—there finding a home, she receives an earthly frame which appears to be self-moved, but is really moved by her power; and this composition of soul and body is called a living and mortal creature.⁸

This is one of the most famous passages in all Plato. It contains the Platonic anthropology of alienation; the theory that the origin of man is in the unhappy separation of the soul from its Heavenly Home. And in this passage also lies the germ of Plato's psychology itself. It derives from the doctrine of the imperfection of the soul on account of which it incarnates itself in the earthly body, and is explained in terms of this alienation.

In brief, a tripartite psychology of consciousness, a theory of alienation of the soul from its original abode, and a negative attitude of rejection of the world, constitute the principal terms in Plato's description of the human soul. The distinctness of the soul, as an immaterial, self-active principle or essence, and the autonomy

---

⁶ *The Republic*, 439.
⁷ *Ibid.*, 440.
⁸ *Phaedrus*, 246.

of the soul as the source of its own powers and activities are emphasized. By asserting that physical life is a process of purification prior to the final absorption of the soul in the World Soul leads not to the idea of unity in life and consciousness, but to dualism. According to the Platonic psychology reason has its seat in the head; the spirit, in the heart; and the appetites, in the lower regions of the body. And Plato's epistemology uses memory (which is identified as recollection) as the mediating faculty between the Ideal world of eternal forms and the sensible world of experiences. In this epistemology man's apprehension of the universals is only a recollection of the Ideas known by the soul before its earthly alienation. For Plato the soul is both autonomous and indestructible. For, he argues, that the soul though created by God, cannot be destroyed by God, because the idea of destruction is inconsistent with God who is conceived of as absolute goodness. Plato's formulations of the doctrines of the soul in all their aspects finally amount to a philosophy of world rejection.

The primary opposition of theoretical interests between Plato and Milton begins to make itself felt in Milton's attitude of life affirmation. It is a powerful and uniformly persisting attitude in all that Milton wrote from his earliest days to his last. It controls every element in the creative art of Milton, and determines his orientations to life and its problems. This attitude of life-affirmation establishes an irreconcilable qualitative distinction with Plato's philosophy of world-negation. To Plato life itself is evil. To Milton life is full of evil, but it is not itself evil; life is positively good and is to be affirmed in every detail from the sensuous (and even the sensual) levels of being to the spiritual plane which comprehends the former. To Plato the whole life-process is to be viewed as a process of purification, and the soul has to purify itself of life. In Milton, only the evil in life, and not life itself, is to be purified.

When Milton speaks in *Paradise Lost* of life being purified to attain through tract of time to the condition of spiritual perfection, he emphasizes the need to discipline and control all the processes of the body and mind, of the world and time, in such a manner that these themselves would constitute not only the prelude to spirituality, but its very content, and become integral parts of that condition.

Raphael's dialogues with Adam in Books Five, Seven, and Eight, are commonly supposed to be one continual lecture on

Platonism. But if we read the passages carefully there could be nothing more "un-Platonic" than the content of these passages, for everywhere in these lines the sensuous plane of life is validated, a validation which Platonism will not brook. The element of spirituality is pointed out as inhering in every phenomenon of man, from the simplest physical acts of eating and procreating to the emotional expression of even erotic love.

True, in denouncing evil, Milton is one with Plato. But in the theory of what constitutes evil, in the discriminations and definitions of evil, they part company. And it is these very discriminations and definitions of evil which constitute the theme of Milton's poetry. It is true also that Platonic imagery is used to denounce and reject evil, but evil is defined Miltonically, and not Platonically. And except for the use of Platonic imagery, Milton's intellectual Platonism everywhere has to be more critically examined than has so far been done. Indeed all puritanism is bad, whether it is from Greece and Plato, or from the Genesis and the Bible. And philosophical puritanism is more dangerous to poetry because it is more insidious.

In brief, *Paradise Lost* is not a poem of life-negation. Poetically it affirms life in all its completeness. What is poetically realized as evil in the poem is its opposite, the persistent determination to view life as evil, and thus to negate it. Milton derives this positive attitude towards human life and the world-process (which is its background) from his carefully developed and reasoned doctrines on the constitutive principles in human nature.

De Doctrina Christiana sets forth both the anthropological and the psychological elaborations on the nature of man. Here, as in *Paradise Lost*, Milton views the drama of life—its comedy as well as its tragedy—in all existential seriousness. In developing his theory of human nature, Milton views man as a total unified existing being. Instead of the Platonic dualism in man, we have here an existential monism, a monism which obviates the distinction in life between this world, and the other world, between the spirit and the flesh. In Milton, as in the Bible, man himself is responsible for his alienated condition in time. The Biblical doctrine of man in this context is quite different from that of Plato. Man's alienation is not the first axiom on which the Bible builds its edifice of thought. Rather, it is on the creation of man which is good. Of the two distinct Biblical accounts of creation, the first one in Genesis 1, 26-30 has no reference to Original Sin at all or to any sin for that matter.

> So God created man in his own image, in the image of God created he him, and male and female created he them. Genesis: 1, 27.

Man here is a generic concept, and no idea of sin and alienation has been introduced here.

In the second account of creation in Genesis 2, 2-7, man has become the particular individual, or individuals, Adam (or Adam and Eve). Even here man is not alienated from God. But it is only in the extension of this account in Genesis 3, 6 that man commits Original Sin, and through this Sin comes the alienation of mankind. So, in the Bible, Sin is that which has come through the fall of man. It has come through man's own decision and action. Life did not begin with it, and it came after life began its temporal career. And though Original Sin has altered life, not irremediably, and has affected the metaphysical status and condition of life, it does not define life itself.

The paradox of Christian anthropology is that man and mankind came into being through God's own creative decision. "And God said, let us make man in our image, after our likeness...." Genesis 1, 26. Milton's comment on this text is, "Previously to creation, as if to mark the superior importance of the world, the Deity speaks like to a man deliberating."[9]

The central terms in the Miltonic and the Biblical understanding of man are the "image" and the "likeness" of God. Human actions are to be ethically and theologically discriminated according as they tend to disfigure and destroy, or as they tend to preserve and reinforce, this image and likeness of God. Man is the image and likeness of God. There is no other postulate more fundamental than this in Milton's thoughts on man. All the thematic digressions of *Paradise Lost* can be comprehended within the meanings of this phrase.

Wherein lies this divine image and similitude? In the soul, or the body, or in both as an indivisible unity? In the soul of man in

[9] *The Works of John Milton,* ed. Allen Patterson (New York: Columbia University Press, 1932-38), xv, 37. This edition is hereafter cited as *The Works.*

"which our likeness to God principally consists."[10] But this soul is neither pre-existent, nor a spiritual entity separate from the body. The quality of "livingness" is manifest only through the body which is alive. To quote Milton:

> So that it was not the body alone that was then made, but the soul of man also (in which our likeness to God principally consists); which precludes us from attributing preexistence to the soul which was then formed, a groundless notion sometimes entertained, but refuted by Gen: ii, 7.[11]

By the soul, then, Milton means nothing more than the "living man in his completeness." A long exposition of this theory from *De Doctrina Christiana* will make his meaning clear:

> We may understand from other passages of the Scripture, that when God infused the breath of life into man, what man thereby received was not a portion of God's essence, or a participation of the divine nature, but that measure of the divine virtue or influence, which was commensurate to the capabilities of the recipient. For it appears from Psal. civ. 29, 30 that he infused the breath of life into other living beings also...whence we learn that every living thing receives animation from one and the same source of life and breath; inasmuch as when God takes back to himself that spirit or breath of life, they cease to exist....Nor has the word "spirit" any other meaning in the sacred writings, but that breath of life which we inspire, or the vital, or sensitive, or rational faculty, or some action or affection belonging to those faculties.
>
> Man having been created after this manner, it is said, as a consequence, that "man became a living soul"; whence it may be inferred (unless we had rather take the heathen writers for our teachers respecting the nature of the soul) that man is a living being, intrinsically and properly one and individual, not compound or separable, not, according to the common opinion, made up and framed of two distinct and different natures, as of soul and body, but that the whole man is soul, and the soul man, that is to say, a body, or substance individual, animated, sensi-

[10] *Ibid.*, p. 37.
[11] *Ibid.*, pp. 37-8.

tive, and rational; and that the breath of life was neither a part of the divine essence, nor the soul itself, but as it were an inspiration of some divine virtue fitted for the exercise of life and reason, and infused into the organic body; for the man himself, the whole man, when finally created, is called in express terms "a living soul." Hence the word used in Genesis to signify "soul" is interpreted by the apostle, 1 Cor. xv. 45, "animal". Again, all the attributes of the body are assigned in common to the soul....But that the spirit of man should be separate from the body, so as to have a perfect and intelligent existence independently of it, is nowhere said in Scripture, and the doctrine is evidently at variance both with nature and reason.[12]

In the propagation of mankind, God does not create a separate soul for each individual. The natural procreation of man involves the begetting of body and the soul together in the living being.[13] The theological argument for this is as follows. If every individual receives his soul immediately at conception from God, then the transmission of Original Sin must also be attributed to God. This is theologically inadmissible, and "If we receive the soul immediately from God, it must be pure, for who in such case will venture to call it impure?"[14]

Thus if we admit that sin is communicated by generation, and transmitted from father to son, it follows that the subject of sin, namely, the rational soul, must be propagated in the same manner. For "it is from the soul that all sin in the first instance proceeds". This is a view completely antithetical to the Greek-Platonic idea of the soul. According to the latter, all the sins originate in the body, and the body is a thing separate from the soul. To support the theory that the rational soul can be propagated by generation, Milton quotes Aristotle :

In confirmation of which Aristotle's argument may be added, the truth of which in my opinion is indisputable....It is acknowledged by the common consent of almost all philosophers, that every *form*, to which class the human soul must be considered as

[12]*Ibid.*, pp. 39, 41, 43.
[13]*Ibid.*, pp. 43ff.
[14]*Ibid.*, p. 45.

belonging, is produced by the power of matter.[15]

Though Milton's theory of man is based on the Bible, he does not wholly ignore the later theological elaborations on man. But all these are subsidiary to the Bible. Even the neo-Platonic synthesis of St. Augustine, one of Milton's favourite theologians, is not much used by Milton in developing his conception of human nature. Biblical and Christian theories on the origin and nature of man rest on revelation. That element of revealed knowledge about man is that he is made in the image and likeness of God. In all Christian philosophers, from St. Irenaeus to Karl Barth, the *locus classicus* in their philosophies of man is the text from Genesis: "God said, Let us make man, in our own image and likeness." All theories of man and his nature are summed up in this simple Bible story of the creation and fall.

The Bible postulates no dichotomy of body and soul. Man is considered as a single psycho-physical organism which is related, in the status of a creature, to God as the Creator. The breath that was breathed into his nostrils at the moment of creation was not a separate spiritual element entering the body. It was that efficacy by which the body became a "living soul", or a living being. Unlike the classical Greek theory of man (in which Orphism and Platonism are the central constituents), the Bible presents man as an animated body, and not as an incarnated soul. While the soul may also in a remote sense be thought of as the vital principle which gives "form" to the body, and as such, may constitute the living being as a whole, it is not to be understood as pre-existent.

Thus in Christian thought the substantial unity of the human personality is fundamental. The tensions between the body and the soul which underlie the Greek reflections on man are completely absent here. But the tensions in the human personality come not from the dualism of the body and the soul, but from sin; and for sin, the body and soul together are responsible.

Milton derives all the principal attributes of man from the doctrine that he is made or formed in the image and similitude of God. We have seen that the concept of dignity is an inseparable attribute, in Milton, of the human status. There are other attributes besides this. The concept of dignity alone does not comprehend all its implications. In Milton's thought there are other constitutive

[15]*Ibid.*, pp. 47, 49.

conceptions. In *Paradise Lost* he telescopes all these constitutive factors pictorially to describe its human protagonists. Adam and Eve are characterized not psychologically in terms of their motivations, but poetically, by descriptively realizing every implication of and the extensions of meaning in the phrase "God's image and likeness".

Across the centuries of Christian thought, from the ancient church fathers to the Reformation, and after, the concept of man as God's image and similitude developed and acquired newer and newer extensions of meaning. In a later chapter we shall see Milton's own additions to the meaning of this phrase. As it developed, different elements were emphasized at different times, although no single conception previously stressed was ever absolutely excluded. Thus this phrase became a "blanket" concept, embracing a theocentric conception of the nature of man, in which every quality and faculty of man, every state of being and condition of life, was explained and correlated with every other. Its constituent assumptions like moral purity, righteousness, the state of bliss, immortality (or at least its hope), man's pre-lapsarian condition of bliss, and wisdom, all these and many more constitute the complex of the Christian doctrine of man. These are among the universal constants of Christian thought. In employing these notions, Milton was not at all expressing the Puritanical theology of the seventeenth century. Indeed, nothing could be farther from truth than to identify the religious contents of *Paradise Lost* exclusively with the Puritan theology of the seventeenth century. The religious perspectives of Milton's poetry on the whole transcend the restricted concerns of Puritan thought.

CHAPTER FOUR

REASON AS AN ELEMENT IN MAN'S DIVINE IMAGE AND LIKENESS

Milton's emphasis on the rational faculty of man is too well known to be pointed out again. But let us look at Milton's use of the faculty of reason in man afresh from the point of view of the theory of man that has been outlined earlier.

Until the Reformation, Christian thought emphasized the power of reason as the definitive element in man's divine image. It was St. Irenaeus who first propounded it in the second century A.D. St. Augustine developed it further and made it one of the major assumptions of his philosophy. St. Thomas Aquinas, with some modifications and extensions adopted the central tenets of Augustine's thought on this concept. So, it is more or less correct to say that, all through the Middle Ages until the Reformation, God's image in man was taken to be man's power of reason. But before we trace the growth of the theological doctrine of reason, let us look into the primary Biblical evidences for the phrase "God's image and likeness", and make some preliminary generalizations.

The primary Old Testament evidence is in the following passages of Genesis: Chapter 1, 26-27; Chapter 5, 1-3; Chapter 9, 1-7. We have already dealt with the story of creation as given in the first chapter of Genesis. In Chapter 5, 1, we have:

> This is the book of the generation of Adam. In the day that God created man, in the likeness of God made he him.

The same idea has been repeated again in Chapter 9, 6:

> Whoso sheddeth man's blood, by man shall his blood be shed: for in the image of God made he man.

It has further been poetically treated in Psalm 8 which deals with the glory of God's creation, and mans' derivative glory as a creature:

What is man, that thou art mindful of him? and the son of man, that thou visitest him?
For thou hast made him a little lower than the angels, and hast crowned him with glory and honour

(verses 4-5)

This last verse is the basic text on which the Christian idea of man's dignity is based. It may also be mentioned that all these passages (except the Psalms) belong to the Priestly writer or the "P" source, in the Bible.

In the New Testament, especially in the Pauline Epistles, Christ is more explicitly spoken of as the Image of God. The difference is that while man is *made* in the image of God, Christ is the Image of God.[1] The two different usages of the "image" of God in the Old and New Testaments need not cause confusion. In the former, the word "image" refers to resemblance. In the latter, it is understood as the perfect correspondence to the Divine Prototype, and the whole concept has been changed from a mere resemblance to an exact reflection.[2]

I may incidentally refer to the Renaissance exegeses of the Genesis, and explanations of the doctrine of the image. Arnold Williams in *The Common Expositor* gives a summary of all these Renaissance commentaries in order to show Milton's debt to them.[3]

These commentaries themselves were only crude adaptations of the image doctrines in the early Christian philosophers. For instance, commenting on the importance of the human soul as that which contains God's image in man, Williams argues:

> Several of the commentators at this point launch into a more or less extended consideration of the nature of the soul. It is only

---

[1] See Col. 1, 15; and ii Cor., 4, 4.
[2] For a general knowledge and the history of both these concepts, I may refer the reader to Professor Norman W. Porteous's article "Image of God" in *The Interpreter's Dictionary of the Bible*, ii, 681 ff.
There is also the excellent and scholarly study by David Cairns, *The Image of God in Man* (New York: Philosophical Library, 1953). My debt to this book is very great, as the number of times I have quoted it will show.
[3] See Chapter iv, "Adam and Eve", pp. 66-93.

natural that they should do so, in view of the enormous interest that attached to the soul during the Renaissance.[4]

On account of the revival of interest in religious thought in the seventeenth century, many similar theological concepts received fresh attention. But what is important to bear in mind is that their "new" interpretations were very frequently not more than alterations and modifications of old concepts and ideas which were already current in many earlier traditions of religious and philosophical thought.

To return to the different doctrines of the image which had become common factors in all traditions of Christian thought on the nature of man, and which find reflections in Milton's prose and poetry, we have to begin with St. Irenaeus (born A. D. 130). He was among the earliest Christian Fathers who discussed man as the image of God. For him there are two distinct elements of the divine in man: God's likeness, and God's image. God's likeness was in the original righteousness which man had before the fall, and this was lost at the fall. But God's image remains in man, and this is his rationality. Here begins in Irenaeus that emphasis on man's power of reason which was to dominate Christian thought for more than a thousand years, all through the middle years, and the Renaissance.[5] Irenaeus's thought is only a rewording of Greek rationalism through Christian terms. Emil Brunner points out this:

This concept of the Divine Reason, in which man, as the *animal rationale*, has a share—through the concept of the *Imago Dei*, as understood by Irenaeus—penetrates into Christian theology itself. To be 'in the image of God' has now become an attribute of human nature; the view now that it is of the essence of rational being to resemble the being of God. Man is now 'also a rational being' as God is a rational being, only with this difference, that God is Infinite Reason and man is only finite reason. The actuality and the relation to the Thou of the New Testament conception of the *imago* . . . has been forgotten and its place has been taken by the idea of analogy. The nature of man is now something quite different from his relation to God; the original

[4] *Ibid.*, p. 76.
[5] David Cairns, *op. cit.*, p. 75.

essence of man, his original nature, is 'rational even as God is rational' and it is no longer: 'to stand in a responsive relation to God'. Communion with God is now a secondary, additional, 'supernatural element', which may disappear, owing to sin, without altering the essence or the nature of man.[6]

It was this identification of man's divine image with one human faculty, the rational faculty, which the Reformation was to repudiate on the theological level. Brunner has stated the main problem. The ultimate theological dispute all through till the Reformation had been whether the "image" refers to a constitutive and structural element in man like "reason", or to the whole reality and being of man, in his responsive existence in relation to God. If the divine image is the same as the fact of being man, then his rationality is a consequence of man's being the divine image. It is not identical with this image.

David Cairns points out that in all Christian writers up to Aquinas the image of God is conceived of as man's power of reason.[7] It is with Luther and the Reformation on the whole that the doctrine of the image acquires a wider and fuller meaning, and this almost amounts to a radical re-interpretation of it. More of it later. Let us continue the theme of rationality in the "image" doctrine.

It is in Augustine's writings that we find the complete elaboration of the doctrine of man's rationality. He extended the meaning of the concept of reason in such a manner as to transform it into a theological virtue, subordinate to faith itself, and closely related to it. It is this interpretation of reason that we find in Milton. It is also this developed and modified concept of reason which was the starting point for the Reformation Theology of Luther and Calvin.

In attempting to summarize Augustine's theories, we will have to overlook many apparent contradictions in his thought. In spite of these contradictions, some main strands of thought emerge from his works. Augustine deals with the doctrine of the image in his work on *Trinity*. Here he argues on the basis of divine revelation. God's revelation of himself has shown that God is a Trinity. And also God has revealed that man is God's image. Therefore, Augustine

[6]*Man in Revolt*, p. 100.
[7]*Op. cit.*, p. 110.

concludes that man is also a trinity, a derivative trinity. His conception of the human personality is based on man as a derivative trinity.[8]

Discussing the structure of the trinity in man Augustine says:

> But we have now come to that argument in which we have undertaken to consider the noblest part of the human mind, by which it knows or can know God, in order that we may find in it the Image of God. For although the human mind is not of the same nature with God, yet the image of that nature than which none is better, is to be sought and found in us, in that than which our nature also has nothing better. But the mind first be considered as it is in itself, before it becomes partaker of God; and His image must be found in it. For... although worn out and defaced by losing the participation of God, yet the image of God still remains. For it is His image in this very point, that it is capable of Him, and can be partaker of Him; which so great a good is only made possible by its being His image. Well, then, the mind remembers, understands, loves itself; if we discern this, we discern a trinity, not yet indeed God, but now at last an image of God.[9]

According to Augustine the noblest part of the mind is the rational and intellectual nature:

> There is then, a nature not made, which made all other natures, great and small, and is without doubt more excellent than those which it has made, and therefore also than that of which we are speaking; viz., which is the mind of man, made after the image of Him who made it. And that nature, more excellent than the rest, is God.[10]

Augustine first locates the image in man in a trinity immanent in the individual, and has thus arrived at the trinity of self-memory, self-knowledge, and self-love. But this conclusion was against his Christian faith which puts love and knowledge of God above self-love and self-knowledge. Apparently this contradiction was over-

---

[8] Book xiv of Augustine's *On the Trinity* deals with man as the image of God.
[9] *On the Trinity*, Book, xiv, Chapter 8.
[10] *Ibid.*, Chapter, 12.

come by Augustine later with the argument that memory, understanding, and love of self are a capacity for the memory, understanding, and love of God.[11]

Augustine does not believe in the theory that through Original Sin man lost God's image completely. Interpreting the following verse from St. Paul (ii Cor., 3, 18):

> But we all, with open face beholding as in a glass the glory of the Lord, are changed into the same image from glory to glory, even as by the Spirit of the Lord

Augustine says:

> He [St. Paul] means, then, by "we are transformed," that we are changed from one form to another, and that we pass from a form that is obscure to a form that is bright: since the obscure form, too, is the image of God; and if an image, then assuredly also "glory", in which we are created as men, being better than the other animals.[12]

Augustine's main teachings on the image can be summarized as follows. Proceeding on the doctrine that the trinity of understanding, memory, and love in man becomes the image of God, only when it is able to love God, he concludes that this love of the image of God to its Source is the only true wisdom. To Augustine "wisdom" is the response of the human "image" to its Prototype. He makes it very clear that the trinity of the mind is not the image of God because the mind resembles itself, and understands, and loves itself; but because it can also remember, understand, and love Him by whom it was made. Thus, beginning with the idea that the divine image is the rationality of the immortal soul, Augustine transforms it to mean man's God-given capacity to know and to love God. Rooted in the conception that man's Godlikeness is in the faculty of reason, he effects a significant transformation in this very conception. His re-definition of reason immediately establishes the separation between the Logos philosophy of Heraclitus, and Stoicism on the one hand with their concept of the essential divinity of man's rational soul or reason, and the Hebrew and Christian

---

[11] St. Thomas Aquinas accepts this position of Augustine. See *Summa*, I, 93, 8.
[12] *On the Trinity*, Book xiv, Chapter 8.

thought on the other hand where reason becomes an instrument for the knowledge of God. Reason, instead of being the divine spark in man, becomes the faculty through which man can know and love God. As such it is subordinate to the faculty of faith. This indeed is the theory of reason which Milton holds. This too is the theory of reason which *Paradise Lost* sets forth.

Let us see how St. Thomas Aquinas adapts this theory to his Aristotelian metaphysics. Generally speaking, he accepts Augustine's main argument, but slightly modifies it to suit his metaphysics.[13] He argues that metaphysically God is Being, and therefore all created things image Him to the extent and degree of their participation in being. But His image is to be found, in the true sense, in rational beings only.

The nine articles of Question 93 of the *Summa* deal with man as the image of God; the main points of enquiry can be summarized in the form of three subsidiary questions. These are: Whether the image of God is in man? Whether the image of God is in every man (including women)? and Whether the image of God is in man as to his mind only? Quoting Augustine with approval, St. Thomas adds: "...there is in man a likeness to God, not indeed, a perfect likeness, but imperfect."[14] He further adds that there is some kind of likeness to God in all created beings, but a "true likeness of image is only in the rational soul of man". For,

> ...although in all creatures there is some kind of likeness to God, in the rational creature alone do we find a likeness of image...whereas in other creatures we find a likeness by way of a *trace*. Now the intellect or mind is that whereby the rational creature excels other creatures. Hence, this image of God is not found even in the rational creature except in the mind. In the other parts, however, which the rational creature may happen to possess, we find the likeness of a trace, as is the case in the other creatures.[15]

Indeed, we have now come to the Christian re-definition of the concept of reason. In classical Greek thought, reason is the spark of the divine in man. In Christian thought, it is only a creaturely

---

[13] See *Summa*, I, 93, 2, and I, 93, 4.
[14] *Ibid.*, I, 93, 1.
[15] *Ibid.*, I, 93, 6.

qualification, a purely human thing, through which the creature can have some knowledge of the Creator and love Him. Rationality is only the divine resemblance in man, and not the divine spark. It is an element of God's image in man. As I said earlier, it is in this sense that Milton uses the concept of reason. In Milton's characteristic use of the concept of reason, we notice its transformation into the idea of God's image in man, expressing itself as love of God, and reason is always distinguished from the Aristotelian, or the Stoic conceptions. In the *Areopagitica*, reason is the image of God:

> ...[He] who kills a Man kills a reasonable creature, God's Image; but he who destroyes a good Booke, kills reason it selfe, kills the Image of God, as it were in the eye.[16]

In two important contexts, in *Areopagitica* and in *Paradise Lost*, Milton appears to define reason in terms of the Aristotelian conception of choice. But the rational power of choice is immediately correlated to faith, obedience, and love. It is not simply the power of choice in the ethical sense of choosing virtue instead of vice, knowledge instead of ignorance. It is always choosing obedience to God, faith in Him, and love for Him. Says he:

> Many there be that complain of divin Providence for suffering Adam to transgresse, foolish tongues! When God gave him reason, he gave him freedom to choose, for reason is but choosing; he had bin else a meer artificial Adam, such an Adam as he is in the motions. We overselves esteem not of that obedience or love, or gift, which is of force.[17]

Here the associations of "reason" with "obedience, love, or gift" are only too explicit to be pointed out.

The concept of reason as the freedom to choose obedience and love is employed in *Paradise Lost*. God the Father, speaking of the freedom given to the angels, argues:

> Freely they stood who stood, and fell who fell
> Not free, what proof could they have giv'n sincere

[16] *The Works*, iv, 298.
[17] *Ibid.*, p. 319.

> Of true allegiance, constant Faith or Love,
> Where only what the needs must do appear'd
> Not what they would? What praise could they receive?
> What pleasure I from such obedience paid,
> When Will and Reason (Reason also is Choice)
> Useless and vain, of freedom both despoil'd,
> Made passive both, hath serv'd necessity,
> Not Mee.
>
> (iii. 102-111)

The parenthetical assertion "Reason also is choice", repeating Milton's own earlier definition in *Areopagitica*, and both echoing the Aristotelian definition of reason in the *Nicomachean Ethics*, amounts to equating reason with freedom, or free rationality. In Milton the equation between freedom and reason only holds in a purely theological context. They are both elements, or the two aspects, of the same element, of God's image in man. In Milton's metaphysics, freedom and rationality as man's constitutive principles of being are one and the same. They are both expressions of man's divine similitude and likeness, and in *Paradise Lost*, they have no meaning except in the context of a theocentric existence in which faith, love, and obedience are absolutes in the human situation.

The doctrinal relevance of this passage from *Paradise Lost* (quoted above) to Milton's chapter on "Predestination" in *De Doctrina* (Book I, Chapter 4) has already been pointed out by several modern critics of *Paradise Lost*. Discussing the possible Pelagian implications here, and rejecting them, Merritt Y. Hughes comments:

> The thought here, however, hardly amounts to a Pelagian profession of belief in man's ability to stand fast without support from God's Grace.[18]

The problem here is not man's moral self-sufficiency. It is related to man's metaphysical status as God's image and likeness. The question is whether man is moving towards a greater realization of it, towards a more complete and fuller representation of its prototype, or whether he is moving in the direction of its own obfuscation and disfiguration. The related problem whether God could have permitted evil has also to be considered not in terms of the moral

---

[18] John Milton: *Complete Poems and Major Prose*, p. 260n.

dualism inherent in the world, but in terms of the mythical structure of *Paradise Lost*. Speaking of the nature of "will" and "reason", God the Father says:

> ...They therefore to right belong'd
> So were created, nor can justly accuse
> Thir maker, or thir making or thir Fate;
> As if Predestination over-rul'd
> Thir will, dispos'd by absolute Decree
> Or high foreknowledge; they themselves decreed
> Thir own revolt, not I: If foreknew,
> Foreknowledge had no influence on their fault,
> Which had no less prov'd certain unforeknown.
> So without least impulse or shadow of Fate,
> Or aught by me immutably foreseen,
> They trespass, Authors to themselves in all
> Both what they judge and what they choose; for so
> I form'd them free, and free they must remain,
> Till they enthrall themselves: I else must change
> Thir nature, and revoke the high Decree
> Unchangeable, Eternal, which ordain'd
> Thir freedom: they themselves ordain'd thir fall.
>
> (iii. 111-128)

As a creature, the essence of man is his freedom; he is thus a reflection of the Absolute Freedom:

> Though I uncircumscrib'd myself retire
> And put not forth my goodness, which is free
> To act or not, Necessity and chance
> Approach not mee, and what I will is Fate.
>
> (vii. 170-174)

As Chance and Necessity do not approach God, so also these should not affect the conditions of man's relation with him. This relationship constitutes his essential freedom and rationality. Both can be comprehended under one concept, the concept of freedom. The constitutive principle of all created beings, angels and men, is the principle of freedom, because all creation reflects, in varying degrees, the Creator who is Freedom. The essential definition of man in *Paradise Lost* is not as a being which has freedom, but as a *being which is freedom*.

Thus every exercise of freedom on the part of the creature has a trace of divinity in it, for thereby it is participating in Godlikeness. A freedom which lacks the content of rationality is sin, and rationality, we have seen, as the divine image in man, is man's power of choice oriented towards love of God. Thus, as *Paradise Lost* develops its metaphysics of freedom, sin can come into being in a world created by God, without God creating sin, or without His being responsible for it. For, Sin is freedom without rationality. The only pre-determination which God enjoins in respect of man, is the predetermination (not of fate) but of freedom. Man is destined or "condemned" to be free, "for so/I form'd them free, and free they must remain,/Till they enthrall themselves." And the "High Decree" which makes human nature, and ordained its freedom is "Unchangeable, Eternal".

The apparent antithesis between human self-sufficiency and divine grace collapses in the poetic conception of man as God's image and likeness. That this self-sufficiency itself is part of the religious doctrine of man on which *Paradise Lost* is based is clear from the text. For the theological orthodoxy of this poetical interpretation of the nature of man, we may turn either to St. Augustine or to St. Thomas, and both substantially agree in their analyses of the Divine similitude in man. To quote St. Thomas:

> Since man is said to be the image of God by reason of his intellectual nature, he is the most perfectly like God according as his intellectual nature can most imitate God. Now this intellectual nature imitates God chiefly in this, that God understands and loves Himself. Therefore the image of God may be considered in man in three ways. First inasmuch as man possesses a natural aptitude for understanding and loving God; and this aptitude consists in the very nature of human mind, which is common to all men. Secondly, inasmuch as man actually or habitually knows and loves God, though imperfectly; and this image consists in the conformity of grace. Thirdly, inasmuch as man knows God actually and loves him perfectly; and this image consists in the likeness of glory. Therefore on the words, *The light of Thy countenance, O Lord, is signed upon us* (Ps. iv, the *Gloss* distinguished a threefold image, of *creation*, of *recreation*, and of *likeness*.

The first is found in all men, the second only in the just, the third only in the blessed.[19]

Raphael expresses the same theory:

> freely we serve,
> Because we freely love, as in our will
> To love or not; in this we stand or fall.
>
> (v. 538-540)

---

[19]*Summa.*

CHAPTER FIVE

OTHER DIMENSIONS OF HUMAN NATURE, AND THE REFORMATION CONTRIBUTION TO THE DOCTRINE OF MAN

MAN'S ESSENCE MAY be grasped as freedom and rationality on the theoretical level. But poetry must set forth its understanding of man descriptively, and through images, and not analytically and discursively. Simply, in other words, a poem which has for its theme the nature of man must embody its understanding of man in characters.

For the delineation of characters in *Paradise Lost*, the later developments in the analysis of man's nature during the Reformation, proved useful to Milton. Since the characters of Adam and Eve are to be poetically delineated in terms of the ideas available from the Old Testament, the Reformation interest in the Old Testament conception of man as the image and likeness of God and the numerous interpretations which this interest provoked provided Milton with the descriptive material for the delineation of Adam and Eve, and for pictorially realizing their state of bliss in the happy garden of Eden.

The importance given to the doctrine of the images in the Old and New Testaments is shown by the enormous volume of commentary on this theme in Reformation theology, especially in the works of Martin Luther, and of John Calvin. In fact the most significant point of departure for Reformation Christian thought from the medieval tradition lay in reworking and expanding the meaning of God's image in man. We are here only concerned with certain strands of thought. The doctrine of predestination in Reformation theology can only be understood in relation to its interpretation of the effect of Original Sin on man's divine similitude. Milton's own argument against predestination is based on his belief that Sin cannot efface completely God's image in man.

In this chapter we shall deal with Luther's contribution to this tradition of thought, and Milton's use of it in *Paradise Lost*. Luther was the first thinker to transform the conception of God's image and likeness from a faculty of man to the whole fact of being human, and the conditions of human life. So God's image in man was not, according to Luther, one quality or faculty like rationality, or freedom, however important it might be. While Luther stressed all those elements in human consciousness which distinguish and set apart the human from the non-human, he particularly laid emphasis on two aspects of human life mentioned in the Bible as distinctive marks of the divine image in man. These are, first, the power which man had before the fall over the rest of creation, his supremacy over nature and his overlordship over the animals; and second, a state of being which combined original righteousness, the blissful joy of life which itself is a complex of several other factors, and wisdom. We shall see later in the chapter how Milton employs these conceptions in *Paradise Lost*.

Luther's commentary on Genesis 1, 26, deals with the creation of man, and on the phrase the "image and likeness of God". He identifies the image in two things in the creation account. First, it is a state of being, a condition and form of life in which moral righteousness is combined with a complete freedom from fear and anxiety. After discussing the views of the Fathers on this, Luther says:

> Therefore that image of God was something most excellent, in which were eternal life, everlasting freedom from fear, and everything that is good....Although we utter the words, who is there who could understand what it means to be in a life free from fear, without terrors and dangers, to be wise, upright, good, and free from all disasters, spiritual as well as physical? However, greater than these was the fact that Adam was fitted for eternal life. He was so created that as long as he lived in this physical life, he would till the ground, not as if he were doing an irksome task and exhausting his body by toil but with supreme pleasure, not as a pastime but in obedience to God and submission to His will.[1]

Man's original righteousness is, according to Luther, a central element in this image. Although in all his important passages he appears to equate the image with man's righteousness, he does not wholly identify this image with it. Other ideas are equally relevant.

[1] *Luther's Works*, i, 65.

But this is the central element which was lost at the fall of man. On the whole, according to Luther, man's pre-lapsarian nature is defined as God's image and likeness by his original righteousness, unparalleled bliss, freedom from fear, and promise of eternal life. Even Adam's daily task in tilling the ground was a pleasurable one because it was in obedience to God and in submission to His will.

There is yet another aspect of this image in Luther's theory. This is the dominion over the rest of creation which man had before the fall. His comments on the Biblical text, "let him have dominion over the fish of the sea, etc." is as follows:

> Here the rule is assigned to the most beautiful creature, who knows God, in whom the similitude of the divine nature shines forth through his enlightened reason, through his justice and wisdom. Adam and Eve become rulers of the earth, the sea, and the air. But this dominion is given to them not only by way of advice but by express command. . . . Adam and Eve heard the words with their ears when God said: "Have dominion". Therefore the naked human being—without weapons and walls, even without any clothing, solely in his bare flesh—was given the rule over all birds, wild beasts and fish.[2]

As a corollary to this, Adam and Eve possessed an "insight into all the dispositions of all animals, into their characters and all their powers".[3] In addition to this knowledge of animals, Adam and Eve possessed, while they were still free from sin, "a most perfect knowledge of God, for how would they not know Him whose similitude they had within themselves? Further more, they also had the most dependable knowledge of the stars and of the whole astronomy".[4] And again, if "we are looking for an outstanding philosopher, let us not overlook our first parents while they were still free from sin".[5]

Milton's exposition of the image in man in terms of wisdom, purity, justice, and rule over all creatures, provides an interesting clue to the continuity of recurring motifs in his prose and poetry.

[2] *Ibid.*, p. 66.
[3] *Ibid.*
[4] *Ibid.*
[5] *Ibid.*

Tetrachordon begins with an exegesis of Genesis i, 27. Elucidating the text, *In the Image of God created he him,* Milton says: "It is anough determin'd, that this Image of God wherin man was created, is meant Wisdom, Purity, Justice, and rule over all creatures."[6]

In the Adam and Eve of *Paradise Lost,*

> The Image of thir glorious Maker shone,
> Truth, Wisdom, Sanctitude severe and pure.
> (iv. 292-293)

The motif of man's dominion over the animals recurs in the epic:

> Let us make now Man in our image, Man
> In our similitude, and let them rule
> Over the Fish and Fowl of Sea and Air,
> Beast of the Field, and over all Earth,
> And every creeping thing that creeps the ground.
> (vii. 519-523)

Again in Book Twelve, in the vision of the future, Adam laments man's usurpation of power and dominion over man, for man was given power and dominion only over animals.

> O execrable Son so to aspire
> Above his Brethren, to himself assuming
> Authority usurpt, from God not giv'n:
> He gave us only over Beast, Fish, Fowl
> Dominion absolute; that right we hold
> By his donation....
> (xii. 64-68)

As Luther says, this dominion over animals collaterally implied Adam's insight into the nature and disposition of all animals, so that he (Adam) had all the qualities of an outstanding "natural philosopher". And according to Milton, it is through this God-given wisdom that Adam was able to name the animals:

> But Adam...had the wisdom giv'n him to know all creatures,

[6] *The Works,* iv, 74.

and to name them according to their properties....
(*Tetrachordon*)⁷

Raphael's description of the sixth day of creation states in poetry the same theme:

> ...the rest are numberless,
> And thou thir Natures know'st, and gav'st them Names,
> Needless to thee repeated; nor unknown
> The Serpent subtl'st Beast of all the field,
> Of huge extent sometimes, with brazen Eyes
> And hairy Mane terrific, though to thee
> Not noxious, but obedient at thy call.
>
> (vii. 492-498)

It is essentially a Lutheran idea that the pre-lapsarian condition of man, the life of Adam and Eve, was one of bliss, crowned with hope of immortality. In Adam, according to Luther:

> There was an enlightened reason, a true knowledge of God, and a most sincere desire to love God and his neighbour, so that Adam embraced Eve and at once acknowledged her to be his own flesh. Added to these were other lesser but exceedingly important gifts... a perfect knowledge of the nature of the animals, the herbs, the fruits, the trees, and the remaining creatures.
> If all these qualities are combined do they not make up and produce the sort of man in whom you would think that the image of God is reflected, especially when you add the rule over the creatures?⁸

Adam had a twofold life, "a physical one, and an immortal one, though this was not clearly revealed, but only in hope. Meanwhile he would have eaten, he would have drunk, he would have laboured, he would have procreated, etc".⁹

The hope of immortality was to be realized in the slow transformation of the physical into the spiritual. Immortality was not a

---
⁷ *The Works*, iv, 92.
⁸ *Luther's Works*, i, 63-4.
⁹ *Ibid.*, p. 57.

timeless extension of Adam's life in Paradise, but the translation of this animal life into the spiritual life. Quoting Peter Lombard's comment that even if Adam had not fallen through his sin, still, after the appointed number of saints had been attained, God would have translated them from this animal life to the spiritual life, Luther says:

> Adam was not to live without food, drink, and procreation. But at a pre-determined time, after the number of saints had become full, these physical activities would have come to an end; and Adam together with his descendants, would have been translated to the eternal and spiritual life. Nevertheless, these activities of physical life—like eating, drinking, procreating, etc.—would have been a service pleasing to God; we could also have rendered this service to God without the defect of the lust which is there now after sin, without any sin, and without the fear of death. This would have surely been a pleasant and delightful life, a life about which we may indeed think but which we may not attain in this life.[10]

On the whole, Luther thus transformed the conception of man's nature as God's image and likeness. His expanded conception of man comprehended the state of man's being (as part of his nature), a condition and form of responsible, responsive, and blissful existence in harmony with God, and therefore with nature, and with himself. For the pictorial effects Milton used these conceptions too in *Paradise Lost*. I am not arguing that Milton borrowed these conceptions specifically for the composition of the poem; but that these conceptions constituted part of the worldview of the post-Reformation Christian, in the seventeenth century as well as in our century. For any one who has a serious interest in the nature of man, and wishes to express his own knowledge of human nature from a religious point of view, either in poetry or in philosophy can afford to be unfamiliar with Luther's enquiries into the religious conception of man. This is specially true of the seventeenth century, and of an author like Milton whose worldview is religious.

So, in Milton, as in Luther, man's divine similitude and likeness lie in the harmonious integration of life on the three spheres

[10] *Ibid.*, pp. 56-7.

of conscious relationship. Along with the previous metaphysical elements of human rationality and human freedom, this expanded conception of the image in man enabled Milton to present the character of Adam and Eve (the "man" of the poem) in the background of his relationship to nature, to his Maker, and to himself.

Raphael tells Adam:

> Be strong, live happy, and love, but first of all
> Him whom to love is to obey, and keep
> His great command; take heed lest Passion sway
> Thy judgment to do aught, which else free Will
> Would not admit; thine and all of thy Sons
> The weal or woe in thee is plac't; beware.
> I in thy persevering shall rejoice,
> And all the Blest: stand fast; to stand or fall
> Free in thine own Arbitrement it lies.
> Perfect within, no outward aid require;
> And all temptation to transgress repel.
>
> (viii. 633-642)

All the dialogues between Raphael and Adam set forth various aspects of man, his origin, and the responsibilities which devolve on him from the facts of his nature. Thus Books Five, Six, Seven, and Eight, re-inforce through narration and dialogue what Books Three and Four describe. Of all the epic dialogues in the central Books of *Paradise Lost*, the most celebrated one is Raphael's lecture on the "scale of being" in Book Five, lines 469 to 490. In a sense, this is one of the most philosophical passages in the poem, and it has been interpreted in several ways.

Metaphysically, the passage expounds the hope of immortality. Ethically it propounds a theory of purification. Philosophically it states the theme of the continuity of all planes of existence, from the lowest to the highest. The passage also incorporates the Platonic overtones of emanation and successive states of spirituousness. There is besides the symbolism of the Tree of Life. The alchemical analogy for the ascent of species through successive purifications too is explicit. But then, What is the theme of the passage? Attempts have been made to read this passage in terms of Plato's philosophy in the

Republic and *Timaeus*. But a careful examination will show that it does not deal with the purification of spirit from evil. In the poetic context there is no evil yet. Neither is matter, nor any of the lower forms of created beings can be called "evil", for there is no "evil" yet, either actually or potentially. The dialogue takes place in Paradise before the fall of man, through which sin came, and evil became a reality. In the condition of Paradise all things were good, having been created by God. The purpose of Raphael's lecture is to rule out even the possibility of evil. The Platonic and alchemical ideas of purification can be here relevant only if we postulate the real presence of evil at this stage in Paradise. Since the poem does not support such a conclusion, the Platonic idea of "purification" of the spirit from evil is utterly irrelevant to this passage. To Plato matter is evil, To Milton (Raphael) and it is not. To Plato earthly life is evil, to Milton (as to Raphael) it is the beginning of immortality before the fall; and Raphael's narrations are before man's fall, and with a view to preventing its precipitation. Then what the passage deals with is the eschatological hope of immortality, which hope was part of God's image in man. In Plato spirituality is attained through the negation of the non-spiritual. The non-spiritual is the material in Plato. But according to the Miltonic dialogue spirituality is attained through the direct translation of the non-spiritual and the material into the spiritual. Thus this passage sets forth the theme of the continuity of life and the unity of being of which man is the crown and conclusion by virtue of his being God's image and likeness. This is the central theme of the passage. It is restated in the lines:

> Wonder not then, what God for you saw good
> If I refuse not, but convert, as you,
> To proper substance; time may come when men
> With angels may participate, and find
> No inconvenient Diet, nor too light Fare:
> And from these corporal nutriments perhaps
> Your bodies may at last turn to spirit,
> Improv'd by tract of time, and wing'd ascend
> Ethereal, was wee, or may at choice
> Here or in Heav'nly Paradise dwell;
> If you be found obedient, and retain
> Unalterably firm his love entire

> Whose progeny you are. Meanwhile enjoy
> Your fill what happiness this happy state
> Can comprehend, incapable of more.
>
> (v. 491-505)

For a gloss on this passage, instead of going to Plato's *Timaeus*, one may turn to Luther's commentary on Genesis 1.26. This could be more helpful. In a passage from Luther already quoted in this chapter, he maintains that the physical processes of natural life, eating, drinking, labouring, resting, and procreating are all to be viewed, not in opposition and contradistinction to spiritual activities, but as part of these. In the state of pre-lapsarian Paradise when man was God's image and likeness the physical was not the opposite of the spiritual. It was the necessary antecedent, precondition, and the beginning of the spiritual. Man's Godlikeness was not in the spirit alone, but in the unity of the flesh and the spirit. The pleasures of the flesh were not simply transcended in the spirit, but comprehended within the blissful life which reflected divine similitude. And all "these activities of physical life—like eating, drinking, procreating, etc.—would have been a service pleasing to God...."[11], till "Your bodies may at last turn all to spirit,/Improv'd by tract of time." In the entire "moral instruction" of Adam by Raphael, there never occurs a puritanical or rigidly Platonic conception of purification through abstention from physical pleasures. The only purification that is hinted at is purification through love and obedience. As Raphael expressly says:

> Meanwhile enjoy
> Your fill what happiness this happy state
> Can comprehend, incapable of more.

"Meanwhile, enjoy your fill" is not the command which a "Platonic" Raphael would give to a human being. The greatest difficulty in interpreting Raphael's "scale of being" lecture in accordance with Plato's cyclic movement of emanation and return (as also with the similar idea of the ascent of the species in the alchemical purification) is that the spirit of the passage is utterly incompatible with Plato's philosophy. In Plato the "physical" or the "material" is a

[11] *Luther's Works*, i, 57.

synonym for the impure or the "evil". Thus all the pleasures of the senses are negative, and are deceptions and snares. So "purification" for Plato implies the complete rejection of the life of the senses, of the physical processes. All human activities like eating, procreating, resting, recreating, etc. are, for Plato, proof of man's alienated condition. But in the Christian tradition of thought which explains man as formed in the image and similitude of God, these very activities conduce to the divine blissfulness of existence.

Raphael says:

> O *Adam*, one Almighty is, from whom
> All things proceed, and up to him return,
> If not deprav'd from good, created all
> Such to perfection, one first matter all
> Indu'd with various forms, various degrees
> Of substance, and in things that live, of life;
> But more refin'd, more spirituous, and pure,
> As nearer to him plac't or nearer tending
> Each in their several active Spheres assigned.
> Till body up to spirit work, in bounds
> Proportion'd to each kind.
>
> (v. 469-479)

From this passage it is clear that all matter proceeds from God in the sense of having been created by God, and not in the sense of having been alienated from God. All matter is created by God to such perfection that each plane of being is capable of. The phrase "If not deprav'd from" shows that evil is not intrinsic to matter, and that it becomes evil only through "depravity", and this comes through Adam's sin. The concepts of sin and of evil are not applicable to inanimate matter, nor to the natural or animal world. These are tainted with evil only through Adam's transgression, and this transgression is nothing but disobedience. Also the lines "But more refin'd, more spirituous, and pure,/As nearer to him plac't or nearer tending" have to be read bearing in mind Milton's notion that the spiritual does not exclude the corporeal and material. The "spiritual" comprehends the latter within a scheme of organization in which every plane of being has its allotted status and function. In every plane "spriituality", or "purity", is attained by the proper fulfilment of the functions allotted to that plane. The next line,

"Each in their several Spheres assign'd" makes this meaning explicit. Further, when "body up to spirit work, in bounds/Proportion'd to each kind..."the body is not rejected, not negated as evil, and is not that from which the spirit is purified, but is that which is transformed into the spirit. The body attains spirituality through the proper and harmonious fulfilment of its task as a "living being", or "living soul". Milton's theory of the corporeality of the angels and the materiality of the spiritual reciprocally implies the spirituality of the material, by virtue of the fact that all matter too has been created by God.

A certain ambiguity of meaning appears to inhere in Milton's use of the words "pure", "refin'd", and "spirituous" in line 475, "But more refin'd, more spirituous, and pure,". But this ambiguity vanishes when we associate these words with the next line, "As nearer to him plac't or nearer tending". So these words "refin'd, more spirituous, and pure" imply only nearness to God, or simply "nearer tending". The idea that matter is intrinsically evil is not at all present here.

The whole philosophy of Raphael amounts to the teaching that the world is good, and to maintain its goodness, Adam must persevere in love and obedience to God whose image and likeness he is. It is the philosophy, not of the *Republic*, nor of the *Timaeus*, but of the text, "And God saw all things that he had made, and they were very good". Luther's comment on this text is:

> After God has finished His works, He speaks after the custom of one who has become tired, as if he wanted to say: "Behold I have prepared all things in the best way. The heaven I have prepared as a roof; the earth is the flooring; the animals—with all the appointments of the earth, the sea, and the air—are possession and wealth; seeds, roots, and herbs are the food. Moreover, he himself, the lord of these, man, has been created. He is to have knowledge of God, and with the utmost freedom from fear, with justice, and wisdom, he is to make use of the creatures as he wishes, according to his will. Nothing is lacking. All things have been created in greatest abundance for physical life...."[12]

This is precisely the drift and direction of Raphael's "Scale of Being" lecture. It implies that while man has been created in

[12] *Luther's Works*, i, 73.

God's image and likeness, God's footprints are seen in the animals too, and in the rest of the entire creation. Or, as Luther put it:

> ...[man] He created according to his own similitude. The rest of the animals are designated footprints of God; but man alone is God's image.... In the remaining creatures God is recognized as by His footprints, but in the human being, especially in Adam, He is truly recognized, because in him there is such wisdom, justice, and knowledge of all things that he may rightly be called a world in miniature."[13]

The final moral task which Raphael propounds to Adam is to diligently preserve this image till it is completed and perfected in that which is not made in the image of God, but *is the Image of God*, and which has already been alluded to in Book Three, Book Seven, and finally shown by Michael in Book Twelve. That is the Image (which is the Messiah) of God the Son.

[13] *Ibid.*, 68.

CHAPTER SIX

THE DIGNITY OF MAN

No ATTRIBUTE IS in Milton's thought more intrinsic to man than his dignity. The robe of dignity covers the complete man, the outer as well as the inner man. But whence is this robe? According to Prof. Grierson:

> the conception of Christian conduct as springing from man's sense of his own worth, a worth conferred by God from the beginning and renewed by redemption, is as characteristic of Milton, nurtured on the Bible, but nurtured also on the classics, as it is alien to the general trend of Protestant thought in Milton's England, which laid more stress on man's worthlessness than on his worth.[1]

This significant observation of Prof. Grierson contains many important points. As has already been argued, Milton's Christian ideas do not spring exclusively from the general trend of English Protestant thought in his century, nor can *Paradise Lost* be understood in terms of the Puritan theology of his time. And as *Paradise Lost* illustrates the creative synthesis of ideas one can discover sources and analogues for Milton's ideas in many places, and sometimes even in the least expected quarters.

Consider, for instance, the conception of human dignity which recurs again and again in Milton's prose and poetry. Many sources, classical, Platonic, and Christian can be traced for the origin and development of the complex of notions relating to human dignity. Herschel Baker's valuable book *The Dignity of Man* (Harvard University Press, 1947) makes an exhaustive study of the development of this concept. My limited aim in this chapter is to show that this concept had received extensive considerations in Reformation theology, and strangely enough in the works of Calvin himself where we least expect to find it, for Calvin's thought is usually taken to emphasize predestination and man's original sin and intrinsic worthlessness. It is not at all suggested that Milton borrowed this idea of human dignity from Calvin. But we cannot

[1] "Milton", *Encyclopaedia of Religion and Ethics* (1955), vii, 641-8.

escape noticing a strange similarity between Milton's use of it, and Calvin's. However, when citations from Calvin and Milton are juxtaposed for comparison and analysis, no idea of Milton's debt to Calvin is specifically invoked. My purpose is to show that the concept of human dignity is not at all extrinsic to Reformation theology, and also that in Calvin's theology too it finds extended application.

Accordingly we have to take the concept of human dignity as one of the universal constants in Christian thought, and that Milton uses it in his prose and poetry (without directly borrowing from any particular individual source) in such a manner as to lend support to the view that Milton's doctrine of human nature with all its component elements can well be comprehended within the Biblical and Christian traditions.

Milton everywhere correlates the conception of dignity, and the nature of man, first to the fact that man was created in a special sense by God, and secondly to the fact that man has been regenerated and ingrafted to His Son, and thereby adopting him to a new fellowship with God. *Tetrachordon* begins with this conception of dignity:

> And that we begin so high as man created after Gods owne Image, there want not earnest causes. For nothing now adayes is more dangerously forgott'n, then the true dignity of man, almost in every respect. . . .[2]

To Milton there is no falsehood more dangerous than a pretended sense of "conscious unworthinesse". Commenting on the want of an equation between natural privileges and inward goodness in the corrupt days of his time, Milton says that men accept a "servile sense of their own conscious unworthinesse."[3] Accordingly, in the pretended humility of men around him in his time, he sees only a self-conscious deception which opposes human and gospel liberty, and thus they pride "themselves in a specious humility and strictnesse bred out of low ignorance. . . ."[4]

Christian dignity expresses itself in lowliness, readiness to serve, and in being patient.[5] In *The Reason of Church-government Urg'd*

---
[2] *The Works*, iv, 75.
[3] *Ibid*.
[4] *Ibid*.
[5] This is T.S. Eliot's humility, the most fundamental Christian virtue.

against Prelaty, Milton sets forth a conception of dignity which later achieved poetic realization in the character of Jesus in *Paradise Regained.* This sense of human dignity is quite compatible with Christian humility. Says Milton:

> For who is thir almost that measures wisdom by simplicity, strength by suffering, dignity by lowlinesse, who is there that counts it first, to be last, something to be nothing, reckons himself of great command in that he is a servant? Yet God when he meant to subdue the world and hell at once, part of that to salvation, and this wholly to perdition, made chois of no other weapons, or auxiliaries then these, whether to save, or to destroy. . . .[6]

The theological roots of Christian dignity and human dignity reach far into the metaphysics of creation. Man has a twofold dignity in that he was made after self-conscious deliberation on the part of the Deity. Man was made by a special act of creation by God. Secondly, man's dignity is founded upon the fact that God himself ransomed him from perdition, and adopted him to a new status of fellowship. The visible effects of the complex core of dignity and glory inform his physical personality, and are visible even in his forehead.

> But he that holds himself in reverance and due esteem, both for the dignity of God's image upon him, and for the price of his redemption, which he thinks is visibly markt upon his forehead, accounts himself both a fit person to do the noblest and goodliest deeds, and much better worth then to deject and defile, with such a debasement and such a pollution as sin is, himself so highly ransom'd and ennobl'd to a new friendship and filiall relation with God.[7]

In *Considerations touching the likeliest means to remove Hirelings out of the church,* Christian dignity alone should qualify a person to be a priest, and fulfil any ministerial function. If Christians knew their own dignity they would banish priests and presbyters,

> Out of which hireling crew together with all the mischiefs,

[6] *The Works,* iii, part i, 243.
[7] *Ibid.,* pp. 260-1.

dissentions, troubles, warrs, meerly of their own kindlings, Christendome might soone rid herself and be happier if Christians would but know their own dignitie, their libertie, their adoption, and let it not be wondered if I say, their spiritual priesthood, whereby they have all equally access to any ministerial function whenever called by their own abilities and the church, though they never come neer commencement or the universitie.[8]

The dignity of the outer man is in the stateliness of his bearing, and the gravity of his appearance, for

gravity consists in an habitual self-government of speech and action, with a dignity of look and manner befitting a man of holiness and probity.[9]

In the characterization of Adam, no single physical detail stands out more prominently than the self-consciousness of his own dignity which, glowing through his body, irradiates it and his presence. No appearance of his in *Paradise Lost*, before the fall, is without its foreshadowings of awe, and glory. Likewise Eve, whose imperious beauty stuns even Satan:

Grace was in all her steps, Heav'n in her Eye,
In every gesture dignity and love.

(viii. 488-89)

One can never resist the temptation to quote Milton's description of Adam and Eve in Book Four which should be the basic text for all humanism:

Two of far nobler shape erect and tall
Godlike erect, with native Honour clad
In naked Majesty seem'd Lords of fall,
And worthy seem'd, for in thir looks Divine
The image of thir glorious Maker shone,
Truth, Wisdom, Sanctitude severe and pure
Severe, but in true filial freedom plac't;

[8] *The Works*, vi, 99.
[9] *The Works*, xvii, 321.

> Whence true authority in men; though both
> Not equal, as thir sex not equal seem'd;
> For contemplation hee and valor form'd,
> For softness shee and sweet attractive Grace,
> Hee for God only, shee for God in him:
> His fair large Front and Eye sublime declar'd
> Absolute rule; and Hyacinthine Locks
> Round from his parted forlock manly hung
> Clustring but not beneath his shoulders broad:
> Shee as a vail down to the slenders waist
> Her unadorned golden tresses wore
> Dischevell'd . . . .
>
> (iv. 286-306)

Human dignity is the image of their glorious Maker. Satan himself recognizes the divine image in man, at his very first view of Adam and Eve. His bitter memories are revived:

> O Hell: what do mine eyes with grief behold,
> Into our room of bliss thus high advanc't
> Creatures of other mould, earth-born perhaps,
> Not Spirits, yet to heavenly Spirits bright
> Little inferior; whom my thoughts pursue
> With wonder, and could love, so lively shines
> In them Divine resemblance, and such grace
> The hand that form'd them on thir shape hath pour'd
>
> (iv. 358-365)

For theological precedents we may turn to the thoughts of John Calvin. John Calvin interpreted the doctrine of God's image in man in such a way as to locate it in man's dignity and glory. The whole of creation reflects the glory of God, but man does this in a special manner, being God's likeness and similitude. Commenting on "God's image and likeness in man", he says:

> For although God's glory shines forth in the outer man, yet that there is no doubt, that the proper seat of his image is in the soul. I do not deny, indeed, that our outer form, in so far as it distinguishes and separates us from brute animals, at the same time more closely joins us to God. And if anyone wishes to include

under "image of God" the fact that, "while all other living things being bent over look earthward, man has been given a face uplifted, bidden to gaze heavenward and to raise his countenance to the stars," I shall not content too strongly —provided it be regarded as a settled principle that the image of God, which is seen or glows in these outward marks, is spiritual.[10]

The general trend of Calvin's interpretation of his doctrine of the image, in Chapter 15, Book 1, of his *Institutes* is that this divine similitude relates to the whole structure of man's being:

> ...the likeness of God extends to the whole excellence by which man's nature towers over all the kinds of living creatures.

Accordingly,

> the integrity with which Adam was endowed is expressed by this word [image] when he had his affections kept within the bounds of reason, all his senses tempered in right order, and he truly referred his excellence to exceptional gifts bestowed upon him by the Maker.[11]

True, this dignity is in the soul of man, but since the soul and the body are inseparable, it shows forth, informs the body, and moulds it, so that as Calvin explains the "image", it becomes nothing but the perfection of man's nature and man's integrity, as illustrated in the dignified glory of man's appearance. "Now God's image is the perfect excellence of human nature which shone in Adam before his defection".[12] With Calvin, the concept of man's nature in its resemblance to God has acquired an inclusive complexity of meaning, a comprehensive frame of reference for the reality of man's individual nature. The nature of man's humanity has not as yet been included in this conception. That is Milton's original contribution.

The idea of human dignity is not at all alien to Christian thought. In fact, more than man's "worthlessness", it stresses

---

[10] *Institutes of the Christian Religion*, i, 186.
[11] *Ibid.*, p. 188.
[12] *Ibid.*, p. 190.

man's intrinsic worth. This idea developed through slow incremental addition from the Alexandrian Fathers till, and including, the time of the Reformation. In the post-Reformation revival of Christian thought, the conceptual correlates of man's divine image and his dignity were the central concepts both for doctrinal disputes, and for the rising intellectual tendency to adapt theological insights to the fast developing tides of humanism. The Christian humanists derived their conception of dignity on the basis of biblical revelation. Milton, for instance, derives the conception of the dignity of human labour from this primary concept in revealed knowledge, that of man's divine image. Adam tells Eve:

> ....Other creatures all day long
> Rove idle unimploy'd, and less need rest;
> Man hath his daily work of body or mind
> Appointed, which declares his Dignity,
> And the regard of Heav'n on all his ways;
> While other Animals unactive range,
> And of their doings God takes no account.
>
> (iv. 612-622)

Milton's Biblical support is in Genesis 2, 15.

Satan too uses the argument from dignity to rouse rebellion. In Book Five, Raphael relates the beginning of the discontent in Heaven. As he says, Satan argues that the dignity of angel has been affronted by the exaltation of God the Son (lines 772 to 802). The "magnific" titles of his followers, after this exaltation, have become empty and devoid of dignity. Their angelic dignity has been affronted. Against this plea, Abdiel's solitary and heroic justification of God's ways with angels (lines 809 to 849) centres around the truth that liberty, equality, and dignity are only God-given facts. God zealously seeks to preserve these rather than to destroy them.

> Canst thou with impious obloquy condemn
> The just Decree of God, pronounc't and sworn,
> That to his only Son by right endu'd
> With Regal Sceptre ....?
>
> (v. 813-816)

Further:

> Shalt thou give Law to God, shalt thou dispute
> With him the points of liberty, who made
> Thee what thou art, and form'd the Powers of Heav'n
> Such as he pleas'd, and circumscribed thir being?
> Yet by experience taught we know good,
> And of our good, and of our dignity
> How Provident he is, how far from thought
> To make us less, bent rather to exalt
> Our happy state under one Head more near
> United.
>
> (v. 822-831)

It is in this context relevant to enquire into the question of the effect of the fall on man's divine image. Milton's view is direct and simple. The fall was not a total depravity in the sense that this image has not been completely obliterated. For, had this been so, then man would no longer have remained as man. Therefore no man is pre-destinated to eternal perdition.

The difference between human nature before and after the fall is in the degree of perfection. Adam's nature was only more (much more) perfect than human nature is now. Even if Adam was "perfect", he was still "mutable", and this mutability, implied the possibility of a perfection beyond perfection which was the hope of immortality, given to Adam by God. But even after the Original Sin, a relique of the image still remains, and this is that rudimentary quality which defines man, even in the fallen state.

Adam's characterization in *Paradise Lost* shows his potentialities of perfection. The fall meant the loss of the principal attributes, like righteousness, blissfulness of life, hope of immortality, dominion over the animals, etc. In *The Doctrine and discipline of Divorce*, Milton refers to the fact that "before the fall... man was much more perfect in himselfe".[13] Milton's arguments against pre-destination in *De Doctrina* (Book One, Chapter Four) is preceded by his theory that some remnant of God's image is left in man after the fall. In the third chapter, "Of the Divine Decrees; General and Special", Milton says:

[13] *The Works*, iii, 396.

For, as will be shown hereafter, there are some remnants of the divine image left in man, the union of which in one individual renders him more fit and disposed for the kingdom of God than another. Since therefore we are not merely senseless stocks, some cause at least must be discovered in the nature of man himself, why divine grace is rejected by some and embraced by others; and this difference may not only be perceived daily in the nature, disposition, and habits of those who are most alienated from the grace of God.[14]

For biblical authority Milton cites the parable in Matt. xiii, where "the nature of the soil is variously described in three or four ways, part as stony ground, part overrun with thorns, part good ground, at least in comparison of the rest, before it had received any seed."[15] In the Lazar-house passage in Book Eleven, Adam laments the sight shown by Michael, and his lament relates to the disfigurment of God's image in man.

> ...Can thus
> Th' Image of God in man created once
> So goodly and erect, though faulty since,
> To such unsightly sufferings be debas't
> Under human paints? Why should not Man
> Retaining still Divine similitude
> In part, from such deformities be free,
> And for his Maker's Image sake exempt?
>
> (xi. 507-514)

Michael's reply to this in the lines immediately following is that this image "forsook them" when man sinned. It only anticipates its restoration in Book Twelve.

In Calvin's theology too, notwithstanding his emphasis on predestination, there are places where he lends himself to the interpretation that a relique of the image is left in the fallen man. David Cairns draws our attention to this in Calvin's commentary on John l. 4-9: "In him was life, and the life was the light of men. . . . That was the true Light which lighteth every man that cometh into the world". About this text, Calvin says: "There is therefore no man

---

[14] *The Works*, xiv, 129, 131.
[15] *Ibid*.

whom some perception of the eternal light does not reach."[16]

What aspects of this image have been lost at the fall? Here Luther and Calvin are in agreement. That aspect of the Divine similitude which ensured the state of bliss has been lost. Man, as created in the image of God, lived in the continual fellowship of God. This fellowship has been lost. It is this fellowship which is summed up in the word "bliss".

As we have seen earlier, Luther had extended the idea of the similarity between man's nature and Divine nature to comprehend a state of happiness, "a condition of life free from fear and pain, and anxiety, within it".[17] Luther comments as follows:

> Adam and Eve, now you are living without fear; death you have not experienced, nor have you seen it. This is My image, by which you are living, just as God lives. But if you sin, you will lose this image, and you will die.[18]

There was thus common agreement in viewing "happiness" as one aspect of God's image in man, among all the Reformation theologians. Milton describes the pre-lapsarian condition of life as "pure bliss". The experiential content of human consciousness before the fall is "bliss", after the fall, it is anxiety and dread. Milton reiterates the motif of bliss in *Paradise Lost* from several points of view. Satan's bitter remorse on seeing the garden of Eden and man in it is

> O Hell! what do mine eyes with grief behold,
> Into our room of bliss thus high advanc't
> Creatures of other mould.
>
> (iv. 358-361)

In Book Three, God surveys with joy his creation:

> ...On Earth, he first beheld
> Our two first Parents, yet the only two
> Of mankind, in the happy Garden plac't
> Reaping immortal fruits of joy and love

[16] David Cairns, *op. cit.*, p. 135.
[17] See *Luther's Works*, i. 60-5.
[18] *Ibid.*, p. 63.

> Uninterrupted joy, unrival'd love
> In blissful solitude. . . .
>
> (iii. 64-69)

In Book Seven, Adam, describing to Raphael, Eve's creation and their first nuptials thereafter, concludes by saying:

> Thus I have told thee my State and brought
> My story to the sum of earthly bliss
> Which I enjoy . . . .
>
> (vii. 512-523)

Raphael's parting benediction is:

> Be strong, live happy, and love, but first of all
> Him whom to love is to obey . . . .
>
> (viii. 633-634)

And this is only a repetition of his first greeting to Adam:

> Meanwhile enjoy
> Your fill what happiness this happy state
> Can comprehend, incapable of more.
>
> (v. 503-505)

Adam's full measure of happiness makes him doubt whether he could ever be ungrateful and disobedient to Him who is the Author of all this happiness, and to Him

> Who form'd us from dust, and plac't us here
> Full to the utmost measure of what bliss
> Human desire can seek or comprehend
>
> (v. 515-518)

To this Raphael's admonition is

> Son of Heav'n and Earth,
> Attend: That thou art happy, owe to God;
> That thou continu'st, owe to thyself.
>
> (v. 519-521)

CHAPTER SEVEN

THE TOP OF SPECULATION: MAN EMBRACES WOMAN

> Let us descend now therefore from this top
> Of Speculation.
>
> (xii. 588-89)

ONE OF THE most vexing problems in all Milton Criticism is the task of precisely determining the nature of Milton's attitudes towards what, for want of a better name, may be called "human relationship". No theory of human nature can afford to exclude the complex phenomena of human relationships. Individualism as a theory of human nature is neither complete nor self-subsistent. It is important in the interpretation of the epic theme and action in *Paradise Lost*. The poem is not an epic of individualism. The specifically human factor in the epic is not the individual nature of Adam, or of Eve, but the "human relation" that they are shown to be capable of establishing or of destroying.

Milton's controversial pamphlets and his prose on the whole seem to lend support to the commonly held view that he is the supreme example of the uncompromising individual and the relentless revolutionary. In him, it seems, are summed up the endless dissidence of dissent, the interminable protest of Protestantism. In a sense this is true, for Milton has set himself up as the champion of individual liberty against human institutions, of family, of social polity, of religion. But this "individualism" has to be brought to terms with the Christian concept of man, which curbs individualism through its insistence on neighbourly love.

Paradoxically, individualistic Christianity itself poses the paradox of human relationship. The individual who seeks justification before God has to acknowledge his accountability for his neighbour. "Love thy neighbour as thyself" is as absolute an imperative as "Love thy God with all thy might and thy strength". The one is not possible without the other. It is this "love for the neighbour" which alone can baptize the individualistic Christian as the Christian individual.

To introduce this question of human inter-relationship is not to introduce the question of Milton's ethics here, but to point out the presence of a real paradox in the Biblical theory of man, which it transcends through the conception of love, the principle of the union of man in the communion of fellowship. The biblical anthropology of the origin of man does not deal with man's origin as an individual. When God created man, in his own image and likeness, "male and female created he them". The idea of relationship among human individuals is coextensive and coterminous with the very idea of man himself. That man was "created male and female" does not point so much to sexual differentiation, for even animals have been created with this differentiation, as it does to the human relationship which follows this differentiation, and is caused by it. So the Biblical concept of man incorporates a nexus of human relationships, and in this too, Divine similitude makes itself felt.

Milton's repudiation of the institutional life of man has to be viewed from the standpoint of his idealism. The ultimate ground and justification for the institutional life of man, the familial, the socio-political, and the religious, is the nature of human fellowship which these institutions can promote and support. But institutions come to be controlled by custom and convention, by tradition and law. Thus they violate the basic principle of fellowship, the principle of love. Human nature is completed by love, not by law. Milton has resolved the whole complex of human relationship into the single principle of love, and it is through this that the individuality of man is reconciled with his humanity.

As Milton elaborates the contents of God's image in man in his epic, love too becomes one of its constituent elements. Man's Godlikeness is manifested in the quality of his love. In *Paradise Lost*, Man's Godlikeness comprehends the active, reciprocal, and effective operation of the principle of love. The relationship between Adam and Eve is as much part of the definition of man as the other attributes. The concept of man as Divine similitude extends to the ideality of relationship. This conception of human nature is what Milton employs in his epic to develop his theme and action. The crisis in the poem is a crisis in relationships, first a crisis in the man-woman relationship, and then in the man-God relationship. Again, it is not Adam or Eve as an individual that transgresses but man. When either of them falls, man is fallen.

The ideality of love and human relationship is, according to Milton, an analogue of the ideality of the relationship which subsists in Godhead, the ideality of the unity in the "graded" trinity of God. This analogue of relationship, God's image in man, is what Milton seeks for everywhere and in every plane of human life.

In the Divorce Pamphlets, the communion of fellowship and the union in love which are obtained in the husband-wife relationship is frequently compared with man's union with Christ. Marriage comes closest to this union. In the *Tetrachordon*, Milton says that marriage "is the nearest resemblance of our union with Christ".[1] In the same context, discussing the idea of marriage as a mystery comparable to the mystical union of Christ with the Church, Milton observes:

> For me I dispute not now whether matrimony bee a mystery or no; if it bee of Christ and his Church, certainly it is not meant of every ungodly and miswedded marriage, but then only a mysterious, when it is a holy, happy, and peaceful match.[2]

Again, the quality of love in all true marriages is similar in intensity to that of Christ for his Church : ".... In marriage there ought not only to be a civil love, but such a love as Christ loves his Church."[3]

In *Colasterion*, refuting the arguments of his opponents, Milton expounds the "mystery of Joy" in marriage :

> Another thing troubles him, that marriage is call'd the mystery of Joy. Let it still trouble him; for what hath hee to doe either with joy, or with mystery? He thinks it frantic divinity to say, It is not the outward continuance of marriage, that keeps the covnant of marriage whole, but whosoever doth most according to peace and love, whether in marriage or divorce, hee breaks marriage lest. If I shall spell it to him, *Hee breaks marriage lest*, is to say, he dishonours not marriage; for *least* is tak'n in the Bible, and other good Authors, for, not at all.[4]

---

[1] *The Works*, iv, 98.
[2] *Ibid.*, p. 99.
[3] *Ibid.*, p. 192.
[4] In *Colasterion*, *The Works*, iv, 263-4.

In *The Doctrine and Discipline of Divorce*, Milton views marriage as the blissful condition that it was at the beginning. It is "the pure influence of peace and love, whereof the souls' lawful contentment is the only fountain."[5] It is the

> pure and more inbread desire of joyning to itselfe in conjugal fellowship a fit conversing soul (which desire is properly call'd love) is stronger then death, as the Spouce of Christ thought, *many waters cannot quench it, neither can the floods drown it*.[6]

The essence of marriage is love and "Love in marriage cannot live nor subsist, unlesse it be mutual", and

> where love cannot be, there can be left of wedlock nothing, but the empty husk of an outside matrimony; as undelightful and unpleasing to God, as any other kind of hypocrisie."[7]

Its essence is that mystery of joy and union "that desire which God put into *Adam* in Paradise before he knew the sin of incontinence."[8]

In citing these fragments from Milton's Divorce Pamphlets, one can only illustrate, without attempting to support or refute, Milton's attitude towards marriage and the problem of human relationship in general. It is not the task of literary criticism to propound an ethical theory. It can only illustrate the recurrence of moral attitudes, and aesthetically evaluate their effects on poetry.

Rejecting all the elements of contract, custom, ritual, ceremony, and convention, Milton has resolved the whole problem of marriage on the level of personal relationship. Marriage is essentially and fundamentally a matter of personal relationship, an "I-Thou" relation in which two become one. The problem of sexual differentiation itself has been subsumed under the aspect of this relationship. In its essential nature, the love of a man for his wife is the love of one human being for another, the expression in a different form of the love for the "neighbour" or the love for the "other person". The fact of

---

[5] *The Works*, iii, pt., p. 394.
[6] *Ibid.*, p. 397.
[7] *Ibid.*, 402.
[8] *Ibid.*, p. 396.

sexual differentiation does not establish a qualitative distinction between conjugal love and "neighbourly" love, but, rather, it only enhances it and extends it to all areas of life. Thus in Milton's theory, Eros itself has been subsumed—but not transcended, for Eros can never be transcended, and it should never be—under the category of Agape love. According to Milton, physical love is not the opposite of spiritual love; "eros" is not the rebellion of the flesh against the spirit, but is itself one form of Agape love.

Thus the concept of the individual does not by itself comprehend the concept of man. The former is to be complemented with and completed by the reciprocity and the collateralness of love. The concept of man includes the concept of men, and mankind, and women. "Man embraces woman too". This collateral reciprocity of love is also God's image and likeness in man. This is Milton's original contribution to the Christian doctrine of the image in man. *Paradise Lost* incorporates this idea in its poetic representation of human nature. In this epic, human relationship, an element of man's divine similitude, assumes the form of its supreme example, the instance of the ideal form of "man-woman" love. When Adam refers to Eve as the "Best Image of myself and dearer half", "Sole *Eve*, Associate sole", and "Daughter of God and Man, accomplisht *Eve*", the sentiments expressed are not merely romantic. They bring to the surface through the romantic vocabulary, hidden doctrinal contents in the poem, the oneness of man and woman. Likewise we have Milton's paean celebrating wedded love which sets forth almost the same theme.

> Hail wedded Love, mysterious Law, true source
> Of human offspring, sole propriety
> In Paradise of all things common else.
> By thee adulterous lust was driven from men
> Among the bestial herds to range, by thee
> Founded in Reason, Loyal, Just, and Pure,
> Relations dear, and all the Charities
> Of Father, and Son, and Brother first were known.
> Far be it, that I should write thee sin or blame,
> Or think thee unbefitting holiest place
> Perpetual Fountain of Domestic Sweets,
> Whose bed is undefil'd and chast pronounc't
> Present, or past, as Saints and Patriarchs us'd.

> Here Love his golden Shafts imploys, here lights
> His constant Lamp, and waves his purple wings,
> Reigns here and revels.
>
> (iv. 750-765)

For a study in the analogous developments of Christian doctrines of man in different centuries, let us compare Milton's theory here outlined with the theory of Karl Barth in our century. Barth deals with the doctrine of creation and that of man as God's image and likeness in his famous work *Church Dogmatics*. The four Parts of the third Volume of the *Church Dogmatics* mainly deal with the theory of man's divine image and likeness. He points out that in the two important references to the creation of man in the Bible, the statment that man was created in God's image is coupled with the statement that "Male and female created he them". Genesis 1.27 says: "So God created man in his *own* image, in the image of God created he him; male and female created he them."

In Genesis 5, 1-2, we have:

> ....in the day that God created man, in the likeness of God made he him;
> Male and female created he them; and blessed them, and called their name Adam, in the day when they were created.

On the basis of these texts, Karl Barth develops his doctrine of man as follows. In all the Biblical descriptions of man in the Old Testament there is no thought about man except as sexually differentiated. But this sexual differentiation is not peculiar to man alone, for animals too have it. So, God's image and likeness is not in this sexual differentiation of man and women, but in the capacity of man and woman in transforming this differentiation, and making it as a basis for the creation of an analogue of the relationship in love which man and woman establish with their Maker, which the animals cannot.[9]

This relationship, as Milton has shown in his song in praise of wedded love in Book Four, is the source and matrix of all other relationships in life. This relationship, according to Karl Barth, is

---

[9] See the Section entitled "Creation as the External Basis of the Covenant", in *Church Dogmatics*, iii, part i, pp. 94-228 (English Translation).

necessary to complete human nature, and without it the nature of man remains on the level of animal nature. Man is man only when this relation is posited.[10]

The only objection to this theory is in the question whether a celibate forfeits his claims for humanity. Not necessarily, in Barth's theory, unless the celibate makes the excuse of his celibacy to cut himself off entirely from the rest of humanity. He develops the full implications of his theory in the rest of the *Church Dogmatics* with which we are not directly concerned here.

Barth says:

> It is in the co-existence of God and man on the one hand; and man's independent existence on the other, that the real and yet not discordant counterpart in God Himself finds creaturely form and is revealed to the creature....
> Only in man does a real other, a true counterpart to God enter the creaturely sphere.[11]

The *Church Dogmatics* develops the theory that it is fellowship with God, the uncreated Absolute, that distinguishes the human creation from the animal creation. It is this purpose of creation which defines human nature and its divine similitude. In the words of Barth:

> ..."Let us make man in our image, after our likeness". "In our image" means to be created as a being which has its ground and possibility in the fact that in "us", i.e., in God's own sphere

[10] A question which arises in this context from the biography of Milton has also to be looked into here. The question remains, Why did Milton decide to marry? His early views on chastity had made him identify this "virtue" with celibacy. If he married against his own better judgments due to the compulsions of nature, then he acted wrongly. Arthur Barker discusses this problem in his *Milton and the Puritan Dilemma* (p. 64), and he concludes that Milton's "vitality made the full acceptance of a doctrine of celibacy impossible." There could never be a conclusion more wrong than this. (If this were true, Mary Milton would not have been in such a hurry to go home to her parents, and leave Milton alone.) One possible answer could be that in Milton's considered view, human nature is not complete till it can establish relationships of love, of "collateral amity", an earthly analogue of man's relationship with God. Marriage is the best form of this relationship. And he decided in favour of married life.

[11] *Church Dogmatics*, iii. pt. 1, p. 84.

and being, there exists a divine and therefore self-grounded prototype to which this being can correspond.... That it is created in this image proves that it has in it its ground and justification. The phrase "in our image" is obviously the decisive insight of the saga of Creation, for it is repeated twice.[12]

According to the Creation Saga, no creature other than man can exist in an "I-Thou" relationship to one another, but "man as such exists in this relationship from the very beginning".[13] This relation is duplicated on the human plane in the neighbourly relation among men, and in the highest form of human relationship between man and woman. To quote a long passage from Barth:

"He created them male and female". This is the interpretation immediately given to the sentence "God created man". As in this sense man is the first and only one to be created in genuine confrontation with God and as a genuine counterpart to his fellows, it is he first and alone who is created "in the image" and "after the likeness" of God.... This God-likeness is not a quality of man. Hence there is no point in asking in which of man's peculiar attributes and attitudes it consists. It does not consist in anything that man is or does. It consists in man himself as the creature of God. He would not be man if he were not the image of God. He is the image of God in the fact that he is a man.... In God's own being and sphere there is a counterpart: a genuine but harmonious self-encounter and self-discovery; a free co-existence and co-operation; an open confrontation and reciprocity. He is this first in the fact that he is the counterpart of God, the encounter and discovery in God Himself being copied and imitated in God's relation to man. But he is it also in the fact that he is himself the counterpart of his fellows and has in them a counterpart, the co-existence and co-operation in God Himself being repeated in the relation of man to man. Thus... the analogy between God and man, is the existence of the I and the Thou in confrontation. This is first constitutive for God, and then for man created by God. To remove it is tantamount to removing the divine from God as well as the human from man.

[12] *Ibid.*, p. 183.
[13] *Ibid.*

On neither side can it be thought away.[14]

Barth proceeds from analogous relationships (in God and man) to the sexual differentiation of man in creation. He points out that in the final and supreme act of creation, the Biblical Witness makes no reference at all to the peculiar intellectual and moral talents and possibilities of man, to his reason and its determination and exercise. It is not in something which distinguishes him from the beasts, but in that which formally he has with them (that is, God has created him male and female) that he is this being in differentiation and relationship, and therefore in natural fellowship with God.[15]

Everything else said about man in the Saga of Creation is subordinated to this, that "he is male and female". And at the same time, "this plurality, this differentiation of sex, is something which formally he has in common with the beasts.[16] Barth proves that:

The only real differentiation and relationship is that of man to man, and in its original and most concrete form of man to woman and woman to man. Man is no more solitary than God. But as God is One, and He alone is God, so man as man is one and alone, and two only is the duality of his kind, *i.e.*, in the duality of man and woman. In this way he is a copy and imitation of God. . . . .But this creaturely differentiation of sex and relationship is shown to be distinct and free, to reflect God's image and to prove his special grace, by the very fact that in this peculiar duality (*i.e.*, to the exclusion of all others) he is alone among the beasts and in the rest of creation, and that it is in this form of life and this alone, as man and woman, that he will continually stand before God, and in the form of his fellow that he will continually stand before himself. Men are simply male and female. Whatever else they may be, it is only in this differentiation and relationship. . .they are human. As the only principle of differentiation and relationship. . .it is the true *humanum*, and therefore the true creaturely image of God. Man can and will

[14]*Ibid.*, pp. 184-5.
[15]*Ibid.*, p. 185.
[16]*Ibid.*, p. 186.

always be man before God and among his fellows only as he is man in relation to woman, and woman in relationship to man.[17]

One more quotation from Karl Barth which will illustrate the central problem of epic action in *Paradise Lost*, in relation to its epic theme:

> The fact that he [Man] was created man and woman will be the great paradigm of everything that is to take place between him and God, and also of everything that is to take place between him and his fellows. The fact that he was created and exists as male and female will also prove to be a copy and imitation of his Creator as such, but at the same time a type of the history of the covenant and salvation which will take place between him and his Creator. In all His future utterances and actions God will acknowledge that He has created man, male and female, and in this way in His own image and likeness.[18]

Barth has arrived at the same interpretation of human nature as God's image and likeness as Milton himself, and quite independently of him. This is not an attempt to show that Milton has influenced modern Christian thought, but only to compare for mutual elucidation analogous doctrinal developments in different centuries. If the creature man was formed in the image and likeness of God and at the same time male and female, then this very image and likeness of God has to be sought for in the fact of sexual differentiation and the purposes it is intended to fulfil. The relationship between Adam and Eve is an analogue of the relation between God and man. And the epic crisis of *Paradise Lost* is both a crisis in man's relationship with God, and at the same time, a crisis in the human relationship between Adam and Eve. The resolution of that crisis is in the reconciliation between Adam and Eve, and then between man and God.

---

[17] *Ibid.*, pp. 185-6.
[18] *Ibid.*, pp. 186-7.

CHAPTER EIGHT

WAS ADAM "FALLEN" BEFORE HE FELL?

THAT HE WAS, is the conclusion of all the respectable critics; or, to be considered a respectable critic of Milton, one must at least hold that view.

No event in *Paradise Lost* has elicited more comment and criticism than the fall of man. It is *the* incident towards which all the earlier developments in action converge, and from which later developments take their origin. In this sense too, it is the crisis of the poem. Other incidents, like man's repentance (Book Ten, lines 1085 to 1105), may possess a greater moral significance. Tillyard argues that this repentance constitutes the crisis of the poem.[1] But Tillyard is mistaking the resolution of the crisis for the crisis. The repentance of Adam and Eve is the resolution of the crisis which is the fall of man. This is the crucial event, and for the space of two Books (Books Nine and Ten) Milton maintains the tension of the crisis. It is resolved only when Adam and Eve with contrite hearts and meek humiliation stand penitent before their Maker.

All interpretations of the fall so far have been either "voluntaristic-psychological" or "ethical-intellectual". While I shall not attempt a detailed criticism of all the separate theories on the cause, nature, and significance of the fall, I shall confine myself to discussing the basic assumptions which shape these theories and lead to their conclusions. The assumption that the fall of man has a psychological cause is common to all interpretations, and with this assumption the search begins for the discovery of that flaw in Adam's psychology which is determinative for the fall. The conclusions differ in accordance with the differences in the ethical preconceptions of the critics. Consequently different theories on the nature of man emerge which explain the fall in terms of this nature. But we have seen that Man's nature in *Paradise Lost* is presented as God's image and likeness.

So, a question even more fundamental than the problem of human nature arises here. It is the question whether it is possible

[1]See "The Crisis of Paradise Lost", in *Studies in Milton*, pp. 8-52.

at all to formulate a theory of human nature anterior to the fall. To put it in different words, Is man's psychology responsible for the fall? Or, Is the fall determinative for the psychology of man? The antithesis posed by these questions is not merely of theological interest but is centrally significant to the art of the narrative in the epic. More of this later.

To quote from a recent survey of the variety of theories on the fall:

> Much of the enquiry into this episode of the fall has started from the assumption that it projects certain familiar human weaknesses into the separate violations of divine injunction by Adam and Eve. Commentators generally agree that Eve's defection results from ignorance whereas Adam's is a desperate act committed in full awareness of its immediate consequences. Although some critics have recognized the difference between the acts of Adam and Eve, they have done little more than to point out what they consider to be the two distinct weaknesses which those acts represent. For Saurat, Eve's sin is one of allowing feelings to blind intellect; for Leavis and Hanford, it is pride; for Diekhoff, a fault of mind, a departure from reason; for Bowra, credulous vanity; for Rajan, insufficient vigilance; for Green, inadequacy of the intellect as a guide to the will. Among the same critics, Adam's sin is variously that of passion dominating reason (Saurat, Bowra, Rajan, Hanford), choice of relative evil for good (Diekhoff), uxoriousness (Lewis), magnanimous sentiment swaying reason (Green).[2]

One may add to this list other celebrated views on the fall which are too well known to be quoted. E.M.W. Tillyard progresses from his theory of Eve's triviality and Adam's uxoriousness (in *Milton*, 1934) to a position of collective human responsibility (in *Studies in Milton*, 1951). He observes:

> My point is that both are virtually fallen before the official temptation has begun....The Fall, then, must be extended back in time; it has no plain and sensational beginning; and the actual eating of the apple becomes no more than an emphatic stage in a process already begun, the stage when the darker and

[2] E.L. Marilla, *Milton and Modern Man, Selected Essays*, p. 28.

stormier passions make their entry into the human heart.³

Since the publication of Arthur O. Lovejoy's article "Milton and the Paradox of the Fortunate Fall"⁴, the search for the cause of the fall has become more vigorous. Milton's handling of this problem in the epic is viewed either favourably or unfavourably. Along with the problems of Milton's epic style, this too has become a central issue for contention, and for the division of Milton critics into two groups, the pro- and the anti-Miltonists. We shall take a representative selection from each group for consideration below.

All the charges against Milton's handling of the fall theme have received classic formulation in A.J.A. Waldock's *Paradise Lost and its Critics* (1947). His criticism is that there is a discrepancy between Milton's intentions and his achievements in the poem. Setting out to vindicate one theme, he has succeeded only in defending its opposite. That there is such a discrepancy has been the substance of an earlier piece of criticism too by Clarence C. Green in an article entitled "The Paradox of the Fall in *Paradise Lost.*"⁵ According to Green, there are two conceptions of Good and Evil in *Paradise Lost*, two ideas of the Right Reason, one dogmatic and biblical in which the Right Reason is the arbitrary will of God, "obedience to which means perpetual ignorance of the issues of actual human life."⁶ And there is another operative conception of Good, or "Right Reason", the idea of the rational human mind seeking knowledge and perfection," a mind fully informed with the knowledge of the issues of actual human life."⁷

In Book Nine of *Paradise Lost*, Green argues that Milton wants to present the first as Good, and the second as Evil. But in the poetic process of representation it seems as though in man's deliberate choice of the second conception of Good, of experience, of knowledge, and of perfection, man is really making the right choice. And what is lamented by Milton as man's transgression is paradoxically the assertion of a right choice. By the so-called "transgression" man does not fall from a higher nature, but rises to

³*Studies in Milton*, p. 13.
⁴*A Journal of English Literary History*, iv (1937), pp. 161-79.
⁵*Modern Language Notes*, liii (1938), pp. 557-71.
⁶*Ibid.*, p. 570.
⁷*Ibid.*

a higher one. But Milton's essential lack of sympathy with the rebellion of man in the epic is incongruent with his own convictions as a humanist. And that is the cause of the grating disharmony between the lofty moral of the theme, and the unsuitability of a primitive myth of creation in which Milton wanted to embody his theme. So the poetic flaws of *Paradise Lost* are so radical that they not only spring from the utter incompatibility of the theme with the form, of the moral with the story, of the symbolism with the myth, of intention with the achieved reality of the poem but they also vitiate the structural disposition of the events, and the characterizations in the poem. Milton, questionless, is on the side of the search for knowledge, for perfection; but the logic of events in *Paradise Lost* makes Milton identify himself with an obscurantist rejection of man's very act of self-affirmation, this constituting man's fall. Green sums up the paradox of the situation:

> Adam's rational faculty then, but not Milton's, though it is said to recognize the good at the same time that it directs the will to choose the evil, as a matter of fact mistakes good for evil and directs the will to choose what to Adam's really mistaken mind is evil but to Milton's mind is good.[8]

Adam turns out to be a kind of "Adam as he is in the motions," for he is a Platonist *malgré lui*.[9]

Transpose the ignorance-versus-knowledge, and innocence-versus-perfection antithesis to a love-versus-moral rigour antithesis, or, to the opposition between the fullness of human life and love and the unfeeling restriction and subordination of man to an Absolute Irrationality and an Arbitrariness (which are almost synonyms, according to Waldock, for Milton's God) and we have Waldock's basic terms of Milton criticism. In Waldock's analysis the presentation of the fall was one of the severest tests for Milton, "In many ways it was *the* test". He formulates brilliantly the doctrine of the fall as follows:

> The matter then may be summed up quite bluntly by saying that Adam falls through love—not through sensuality, and not through uxoriousness, not (above all) through gregariousness—but through

[8] *Ibid.*, pp. 570-1.
[9] *Ibid.*

love as human beings know at its best, through true love, through the kind of love that Raphael has told Adam

> is the scale
> By which to heav'nly Love thou
> may'st ascend
>
> (viii. 591-92)[10]

If we are in search for a single factor in Adam which precipitated his fall, then Waldock is right in emphasizing that "love" is that quality. Apart from the recurrence of the love motif in Adam's utterance in Book Nine, we have Milton's own statement in prose in the argument prefixed to this Book that Adam resolves "through vehemence of love to perish with her (Eve)." So long as we insist on asking the question, What makes Adam fall? and in tracing the answer to a quality of human nature, antecedent to the fall, the answer must irrefutably be Waldock's, namely, that it is "love" and nothing else. The fallacy is not in the answer, but in the question itself. It is the right answer to the wrong question.

According to Waldock, the nature of the myth elicits from Milton, at this crisis of the narrative, poetic comments which denounce the expressions of love, which therefore militate against the very nature and spirit of man. In all human situations there is nothing higher than the expression of love, and Milton (as the logic of the narrative inevitably leads) puts Adam in the wrong, nay, more than that, designates as fall that which is the highest expression of the human spirit, love. In other words, Milton's theme and his poetic myth are incompatible. Waldock says:

> *Paradise Lost* cannot take the strain at its centre, it breaks there, the theme is too much for it.... The myth of the Fall was dangerous, and the more intensely it was imagined the more dangerous it became.[11]

Earlier, we have seen Waldock's assumption that Milton selected this myth to embody his theme of love due to an essential limita-

[10]Waldock, *op. cit.*, p. 51.
[11]*Ibid.*, p. 56.

tion, i.e., Milton's want of experience in assessing the suitability of a given narrative for a specific theme. We, in our time, due to our knowledge of the technique of fiction, possess this ability which Milton was without. So *Paradise Lost*, in his conclusion, is an artistic failure.

To the anti-Milton critics, the "fall" is the result of a certain positive causation. The instincts and the motives which led man to violate an arbitrary fiat are good. The "Fall" was no fall at all, but, on the contrary, it was the first significant step taken by man towards self-discovery and self-fulfilment. The "perverse" logic of the Biblical narrative, they say, makes Milton view the "fall" negatively. Milton the poet creates the most poetic of all situations, but simultaneously Milton the Biblical fundamentalist denounces the poet. That Milton was not able to detect the flaw at the centre of the myth of creation, the disharmony between an act of self-realization on the part of Adam and Eve, and the theological insistence on designating as "sin" or "fall" that very characteristically human act of self-affirmation, through knowledge, wisdom and love, was due to the defect of Milton's imagination and his lack of experience in analysing human emotions. This is the sum and substance of the charges levelled against Milton's handling of the myth of creation by those critics who see in *Paradise Lost*, in addition to serious stylistic defects, the incongruence between theme and myth, and the radical structural flaw which this incongruence generates. Reference has already been made to the vigorous efforts at repudiating these negative criticisms. I have referred to Tillyard's sustained enquiry into the cause of the fall and the nature of man in *Paradise Lost*.[12] Tillyard's views are too well known to be discussed in detail here; besides, these have already been subjected to careful scrutiny. But one of his arguments seems to be so self-contradictory as to vitiate his whole position and the conclusion emerging therefrom. Says he:

> The Fall, then, must be extended back in time; it has no plain and sensational beginning; and the actual eating of the apple becomes no more than an emphatic stage in a process already begun, the stage when the darker and stormier passions make their entry into the human heart.[13]

[12] See *Studies in Milton*.
[13] *Studies in Milton*, p. 15.

If this be true, then Adam was fallen at the time of creation itself, and human nature was corrupted from the very beginning. Logically, therefore, it follows that man had no freedom of will, for, according to Tillyard, his will had acquired a propensity towards evil from the very earliest stage itself. This assumption is illogical and untrue to both the text of *Paradise Lost*, and the Genesis myth.

All theories of the fall in *Paradise Lost* are efforts to reconcile the seeming antinomy between freedom as the constitutive principle of human reality and the compulsive propensities in human nature which precipitate action. If the fall is in consequence of any psychological tendency in Adam and Eve, then human nature by virtue of the presence of these tendencies is not free. The fall is pre-determined by the forces present in Adam's mind from the very beginning, and is thus not a free act. But if the fall is not a free act, then its moral responsibility is not on man. And its epic interpretation is not poetic in that that it does not create a new dimension of meaning. A psychologically pre-determined fall with its own laws of internal causation is not Milton's epic theme. The primeval etiological fall is wholly and completely a free act, even when the fall is engineered by the Devil through his temptations. This free act of the fall which is no less heroic than any other is the central episode around which the epic plot is woven by Milton. The fall is not one of the incidents in the epic plot, not a sequential incident, in a chain of antecedents for which the poetry supplies the causal connection. It is *the* event which determines the ordering of all other incidents constituting the narrative of the poem, and which provides the perspective in which these incidents are to be interpreted and assessed.

One of the most important developments in Milton criticism in the middle of our century is the increasing emphasis directed to the theme of the fall in *Paradise Lost*, something which had been ignored by most critics, except in occasional pronouncements. Milton's creative genius illustrates itself in operation, not so much in the stylistic effects produced, not so much in the poetic characterization of Satan, not so much in the lyrical and pictorial power of the best parts of *Paradise Lost*, as in creating the plot of the epic action through elaborating, enriching, and re-working the Genesis myth of creation. The poet in Milton (as *Paradise Lost* shows) is essentially the poet (the maker) of his plot. Here imagination and speculation, intuition and intellection, all fuse themselves into a shaping power of creativity operating in the matrix of universal knowledge in Milton's mind. Here, intelligence and sensitivity combine to produce an interpretation of man. The principal datum in that interpretation is the fall of man. To fully appreciate the scope and depth of the achievements of contemporary Milton criticisms, we have to subject to scrutiny a few more of the important analyses of the theme of the fall in *Paradise Lost*. All these studies attempt to establish the adequacy of these motivations for the fall. Critics may disagree in respect of their conclusions as to the exact nature of the epic motivation in Adam and Eve, but apart from this disagreement they do not doubt the adequacy of the mental cause to the physical consequence of the fall, in which adequacy they see Milton's vindication of God's ways to man.

C.S. Lewis's statement that "Eve fell through Pride",[14] and "Adam fell by uxoriousness",[15] has the essential (and the only) virtue of brevity. His analysis, if any, of the action in *Paradise Lost* does not lead the reader any further towards a defence of Milton than these insights. According to John S. Diekhoff: "...Eve's is a fault of mind; her fall, like all sin, is a departure from reason".[16] Eve's sin indicates defilement of will and conscience, her disobedience is deliberate, and as Diekhoff argues further, "intention is everything and Eve's intention must be to disobey."[17] Eve typifies woman-kind. "In the effective point of the temptation, the aspiration to Godhead, she stands for the race."[18] Hybris is the main motivation in this aspiration, and so the fall is accounted for in terms of hybris by Diekhoff.

Many critics relate the fall to the typical theme of temptation in Milton, thereby heavily loading his poetry with an obtrusive moral content. When, for instance, J.H. Hanford, insists that "the essential fall occurs when passion predominates over reason",[19] the crisis in the poem is viewed against the background of a moral lapse at the centre of the epic action. The epic plot illustrates the theme that the supremacy of human reason ordains his felicity. If this argument is true, then the line which divides passion and love

[14] *A Preface to Paradise Lost*, p. 125.
[15] *Ibid.*, p. 126.
[16] *Milton's Paradise Lost. A Commentary on the Argument*, pp. 69 ff.
[17] *Ibid.*
[18] *Ibid.*
[19] *A Milton Handbook*, p. 233.

in *Paradise Lost* is a thin one. And since paradoxically, the poem does illustrate the supremacy of love, in so far as the author condemns this very supremacy of love, his is a questionable thesis.

The same comments are transposed by Douglas Bush to the context of man's duty to love God. Adam loves his fellow creature (Eve) through the compulsion of female charm. But man's free nature ought to be directed not to the love of created beings, but to the Creator. In this misdirection, says Douglas Bush, is the original transgression.

> Both man and woman well-meaning as they were, had lacked that entire and humble love of God which would have strengthened their moral judgement and moral will against two of the most universal and insidious dangers of human life, ambitious pride and sexual love.[20]

Bush sees in the fall, a moral crisis for man, the conflict between the "apparent" good and the "real" good, which, on the basis of Hooker's theology, he shows to be a rejection of Right Reason. But the poem does not support the theory of abstract good. *Paradise Lost* is not ethics, but poetry, and as such it has a logic of its own. Accordingly the transgressive action of Eve, followed by that of Adam, does not generate in the reader's mind an ambivalent response. The crisis of the action, and the epic comments elicit a coherent attitude. Whether it produces a coherent response or not has been questioned. But those who see a divergence between Milton's moral purpose, and the expression of his instinctual sympathies in the poem do so because of their own ethical preoccupations.

Herbert J.C. Grierson formulates his doctrine of the divergence between moral purpose and poetic achievement as follows:

> Milton has not woven his teaching into the mythical texture of his poem. The argumentative portion is adventitious. It is as if Shakespeare had told the story of Othello in such a way as to enlist our sympathies for the super-human cunning of Iago and thought to save the situation by choral odes or monologues in which he denounced Iago.[21]

[20]*Paradise Lost in our Time*, p. 84.
[21]*Criticism and Creation*, p. 42.

Such a view is the logical consequence of a wrong premise that Milton wanted to render the transgression of man condemnatory, but failed to do so because the motivations which precipitate this transgression are praiseworthy.

All humanistic (like the Platonic theories of the fall) explanations locate the motivations in the wrong assertion of self-sufficiency. "The human fall," says M.M. Mahood (in *Poetry and Humanism*).

> like that of angels, is an assertion of self-sufficiency, but Eve's action is differently motivated from that of Adam, according to the psychological differences of their natures as man and woman.[22] The neo-Platonic antithesis between love of knowledge as an absolute good, and love of oneself as a relative evil has been applied to the explication of the enigma of the fall.

In *Answerable Style*, Arnold Stein sees the fall of Adam (which is the most important element in man's transgression, and not that of Eve) in the tendency towards self-love. Love is the main motif in the theme of the fall. But the love of Adam in the act of transgression is selfish, and self-directing. Thus, at the fall, selfishness masquerades itself as love. For

> In loving Eve, Adam is not really loving his very self. He is loving *himself* as her, not loving her as himself.... Adam can neither love himself adequately nor love Eve as himself unless he can love God adequately.... and so make his love for Eve, the unity of their shared self, an expression of that higher love.[23]

This self-love constitutes the fall itself according to Stein:

> Adam's loving himself as Eve is a false myth of self-transcendence that is tested and exposed by the drama. The self that is defined is avoiding the higher responsibility of freedom to accept a debased existence founded and centred on the creaturely self.[24]

The self-love of Eve shows itself as aspiring to God-head. Both forms of self-transcendence are false directions of human will, compelled

---
[22] *Poetry and Humanism*, p. 218.
[23] *Answerable Style*, p. 115.
[24] *Ibid.*, p. 116.

by the essential weaknesses of human nature.

In "the Central Problem of Paradise Lost",[25] E.L. Marilla advances a more or less similar position. Assuming that the ultimate point of reference in the poem is the social order of fallen mankind, and that Milton is here, as everywhere else, concerned about the moral and intellectual laws operating in this order and shaping man's course in the world, he concludes,

> ...the sin in the Garden of Eden as Milton depicts this sin was the result of what was generally regarded in Renaissance thought as the source of all human failure on a grand scale—man's misconception of his own nature and, hence, misconception of his basic needs.[26]

The defection, according to him, arises from the incompatibility between man's limited abilities, and the illimitability of his utopian aspirations. *Paradise Lost* has thus a serious humanistic purpose, and it demonstrates the terrifying conditions to which utopian ventures inevitably lead.[27]

Retrospectively, the fall can be viewed tragically as a fatal error on the basis of human history, or eschatologically as a necessary step in the progressive revelation of God to man. In the latter case the fall is a paradox, and its mysterious character can be apprehended only in terms of simultaneous antitheses. The fall was an evil act, but a necessary one. It was a deliberate and wilful disobedience on the part of man, but a disobedience which co-operated with the scheme of divine revelation. It was the first cause of man's suffering, but without it the fullness of joy would not have been within man's reach. One could extend the terms of the antithesis almost indefinitely. To apprehend the fall as good and evil simultaneously as the beginning of man's eschatological hope beyond history, and at the same time as man's first transgression in history, is the essence of the doctrine of the fortunate fall. In Arthur O. Lovejoy's theory of the paradox of the fortunate fall,[28] history is balanced against eschatology; the "historical" judgement of the fall as vicious is moderated by the hope and vision of a future

[25] *Milton and Modern Man,* p. 30.
[26] *Ibid.,* p. 49.
[27] *Ibid.,* pp. 49-51.
[28] See "Milton and the Paradox of the Fortunate Fall" in *A Journal of English Literary History,* iv (1937), pp. 161-79.

beyond time. According to him the "Paradox of the Fortunate Fall" has found recurrent expression in the history of Christian religious thought. The idea was no invention or discovery of Milton's. And

> for writers whose purpose like Milton's was a religious interpretation of the entire history of man, the paradox served, even better than the simple belief in a future millennium or celestial bliss, to give to that history as a whole the character, not of tragedy, but of divine comedy.[29]

It is true, where there is sin, grace abounds too. The textual evidence in Book Twelve (lines 469-478) lends partial support to his position. Adam is amazed at the immense and infinite goodness of God, which turns all evil to good. This re-creating of evil into good is more wonderful, as Adam sees it, than the first act of creation which brought forth light out of darkness. Adam now is at a loss to lament over his dereliction or to rejoice: "Much more, that much more good thereof shall spring,/To God more glory, more goodwill to Men/From God, and over wrath grace shall abound." This text lends some support to Lovejoy's theory. And we must notice, Adam's tone of exultation is not accidental, and occasional. It is a permanent feature of Milton's understanding of life in the epic which excludes all possibilities of pessimism. If we read *Paradise Lost* in the restricted perspective of the Puritan theology of the seventeenth century, and of its vision of a reformed society in history, one is misled into identifying the prevailing tone of the poem with pessimism.

E.M.W. Tillyard could never be more wrong than when he locates pessimism in the lines

> Truth shall retire
> Bestuck with sland'rous darts, and works of Faith
> Rarely be Found: So shall the World go on,
> To good malignant, to bad men benign,
> Under her own weight groaning, till the day,
> Appear of respiration to the just. . . .
>
> (xii. 535-540)

Tillyard identifies the major religious emotions of the epic with those

[29] *Ibid.*, p. 163.

of Puritan theology—a stern rejection of the historical process, and an eager longing towards the millennium.[30] The theory of the happy guilt and of the "fortunate fall" of Adam is thus an effective corrective to such an erroneously restricted reading of *Paradise Lost* as that of Tillyard. If there is anything utterly alien to the spirit of the poem, it is pessimism. One must not mistake the tragic sense for pessimism; the fact that *Paradise Lost* can be viewed in Lovejoy's phrase as a "divine comedy",[31] does not minimize the tragic implications of the fall. At the moments when the fall is dramatically realized in Book Nine (lines 734-855 and 990-1016), it has neither the associations of "divine comedy" nor of pessimism. The energy of poetic creation posits the act as a mystery in all its immediacy: the responses elicited are tragic in the sense that we feel immediately the heavy impact of a total calamity, but they defy analysis and categorization.

Even if one finds it difficult to agree wholly with Lovejoy's theory of the "fortunate fall", one notices everywhere in *Paradise Lost* this undertone which redeems it from pessimism. But the doctrine of the happy fall does not explain the fall; it only qualifies it as a happy and "prosperous event", *a felix culpa*.

Man's fall in *Paradise Lost* has to be explained, not in terms of human psychology, but in terms of the structure of the narrative. Any criticism which undermines its structural importance violates the integral unity of the poem.

In fact, that the nature of the fall cannot be explained in terms of the nature of man has already been noticed earlier. But to postulate the fall as a necessary event in the divine scheme of things, in God's plan for perfecting human nature, is to introduce a metaphysical inevitability to the conception of the fall. It only transfers the cause of the fall from man to God; replaces psychology with theology in the determination of it. For instance, Millicent Bell argues:

> Inherent in Milton's ancient material is the paradox of the essential causelessness of the Fall....In terms of the story, we cannot imagine any reason why Adam and Eve should, in the face of repeated warning, have violated God's injunction, not, that is, if we conceive the father and the mother of the human race to

[30]See "Theology and Emotion in Milton's Poetry", *Studies in Milton,* p. 16ff.
[31]"Milton and the Paradox of the Fortunate Fall", *op. cit.*, p. 163.

have been unfallen before the Fall.[32]

All possible explanations only appeal to impulses characteristic of fallen mankind. The fable of innocence and transgression only explains the familiar in terms of the unfamiliar by relating the fallen condition of man with which we are familiar, and the pre-fall condition of innocence and bliss with which we are not familiar through the story of the first temptations of Adam and Eve.

Thus, according to this critic, the fall is only a "causeless" paradox at the beginning of history and, though done by man, it is not caused by his nature. But when the same critic proceeds to the conclusion,

> As Man must be a creature capable of temptation, so the universe at large requires the existence of evil, or at least of potential evil ... .God permits sin because it calls forth his goodness and makes the victory of virtue still more glorious than it would be otherwise, just as the penitence and redemption of fallen Man and Woman opens the way to their more resplendent future.[33]

The theological doctrine of the fall is transformed into a cruel joke and Milton's Satan is more vindicated than his God.

So, the problem of problems in the criticism of the relation between Milton's theology and his poetry is that of determining the nature of the fall of man in the context of human nature. The fall is not determined by human nature. Both the fall of man, and the nature of man have to be comprehended within the scheme of God's creation of man, and the continuous manifestation of God's love for man. The fable of the fall must justify its poetic relevance and adequacy in the epic narrative of *Paradise Lost*. In the epic, it is man that falls, and while he is responsible for it as a free being, the fall itself is not caused by human nature nor by the divine scheme. If the fall is not caused by human nature, neither is human nature determined by the fall. The fall is sin, and it is axiomatic in theology that sin cannot create or recreate human nature. Man as God's image and likeness has his nature in this very fact of being the likeness of God, being created by Him. Sin may alter its condition,

---

[32]"The Fallacy of the Fall in *Paradise Lost*", in the *Publications of the Modern Language Association of America,* lxviii (1953), p. 863.
[33]*Ibid.,* p. 862.

pervert its aim, and misdirect its goal, may eclipse God's image in man, but cannot annihilate this image as it cannot create man. To define human nature in terms of the fall is as fallacious as the other assumption that the fall was caused by human nature, for that would amount to investing sin with a creative power equal to God's. While human nature is sinful, sinfulness is not identical with man's nature, nor is it the principal term in the religious definition of man. This principal term is God's "likeness". The relation between man and his fall, between God's "likeness" in man and its eclipse, is a dialectical one. The narrative structure of *Paradise Lost* eleborates the dialectics of the divine likeness and image in man and its eclipse in him, and the possibility of its restoration within time itself. This is at the centre of the plot of *Paradise Lost*.

CHAPTER NINE

A LITERARY THEORY OF MYTH AND HISTORY

THE MAIN CRITICISM of Milton's use, in *Paradise Lost* of the Genesis myth is directed against this myth itself. As a primitive myth, it is supposed to be unsuitable for representing all the complexities of human nature. The myth's concern with human reality is limited on the whole, and therefore, it is often argued that the myth cannot explore the interior world of man's feelings and emotions. The choice of this myth for use in *Paradise Lost* argues, on the part of Milton, great limitations. These charges thus pose the whole problem of the relation between myth and life, between poetry and history, in a larger critical perspective.

According to positivistic and scientific thought, the myth is false and has no relation to reality, and is just a story for entertainment. At best, it can only yield dubious allegorical interpretations of certain truths now known to mankind as universal facts of life but whose nature was apprehended in primitive days only figuratively.

For nineteenth-century mythographers, and philologists as also for twentieth-century psychologists and anthropologists, the myth acquired some validity as a source of knowledge. The myths in their interpretations became primitive verbalisations of archetypal and prototypal patterns of thought and experience.

It is not in any of these senses or with any of these associations that the word "myth" is used here. Anthropological, mythographical, and psycho-analytical associations have been excluded from our use of the term. We use it here in a strictly literary sense of a narrative structure. In this sense, the myth embodies a perception of reality, and an understanding of life. As the verbal expression of a creative understanding of life, it is neither pre-logical, nor paralogical. And it does not belong to the pre-scientific or pre-logical stage of human thought. Far from this, it is co-extensive with scientific and philosophical thought, and is an alternative to these as a creative, literary systematisation of the experiential reality of man. The literary and poetic use of the form of the myth to express its understanding of life can claim an equal validity with, if not greater than, that of philosophic thought itself. Milton's reworking of the material of the myth for the story of his epic will become clear when we approach the myth from this literary point of view.

The literary myth is the presentation of reality as a structure, and not as a process. By this it is not meant that the elements of change and development are excluded from the purview of the literary myth. On the other hand, the whole complex of human nature, and its relation to the world of Becoming around, and that of Being above, are to be sought under the aspects of structural relationships, and these very structural relationships explain the processes of reality. The poetic myth has therefore to be understood structurally, and not processively. It is this meaning of the concept of the myth, as developed by Ernst Cassirer, that I am partly emphasising here, and not the anthropological extensions of its meaning.

The "myth", according to Cassirer, "combines a theoretical element and an element of artistic creation".[1] Thus the myth has a perceptual structure, and a conceptual structure.[2] In his *An Essay on Man*, Cassirer develops a theory of the myth in terms of its perceptual contents. The perceptual structure of the myth is different from the conceptual structure of scientific, logical, and philosophic thought. There is a mode of perception peculiar to the mythic view of reality. On the distinction between the scientific and mythic mode of perceptions, Cassirer says:

> Mythical perception is always impregnated with some emotional qualities. Whatever is seen or felt is surrounded by a special atmosphere—an atmosphere of joy or grief, of anguish, or excitement, or exultation or depression. Here we cannot speak of "things" as a dead or indifferent stuff. All objects are benignant or malignant, friendly or inimical, familiar or uncanny, alluring and fascinating or repellant and threatening. We can easily reconstruct this elementary form of human experience, for even in the life of the civilized man it has by no means lost its original power. If we are under the strain of a violent emotion we have still this dramatic conception of all things. They no longer wear

[1] *An Essay on Man*, p. 75.
[2] *Ibid.*

their usual faces; they abruptly change their physiognomy; they are tinged with the specific colour of our passions, of love, or hate, of fear or hope... . All the efforts of scientific thought are directed to the aim of obliterating every trace of this first view. In the new light of science mythical perception has to fade away. But that does not mean that the data of our physiognomic experience as such are destroyed or annihilated... . In our human world, we cannot miss them, they maintain their place and significance. In social life, in our daily intercourse with men we cannot efface these data... . While science has to abstract from these qualities in order to fulfil its task, it cannot suppress them... . Science delimits this objectively, but it cannot completely destroy this reality. For every feature of our human experience has a claim to reality.[3]

The mythical perception emphasizes "feeling-qualities", as the basic elements of personality. Consequently, we can never analyse myth into ultimate conceptual elements. For, the principle of the myth is a vital and not a static one. "The real substratum of myth is not a substratum of thought but of feeling."[4] The mythic perception of feeling-qualities leads to a view of reality as a formal structure of relations, and not as a process of causes and consequences. The "myth-versus-science" controversy ultimately boils down to a "form-and-structure-versus-cause-and-consequence" antithesis. To Cassirer: "The concept of form and the concept of cause constitute the two poles upon which our understanding of the world rotates."[5]

The mythical worldview is dominated by ideas of form and structure, as the philosophical and scientific worldview is dominated by the idea of cause. From very ancient times, as soon as the concepts of form and cause were rigorously interpreted, they began to oppose themselves mutually.[6] In *The Logic of the Humanities,* Cassirer deals with the history of this opposition between causal thouhgt from Greek philosophy till our time, and how each of these concepts of form and cause influenced even the history of science.

The essential difference is one between "structural thinking"

[3] *Ibid.,* pp. 76-7.
[4] *Ibid.,* p. 81.
[5] *The Logic of the Humanities,* p. 159.
[6] *Ibid.,* p. 160.

and "causal thinking". In pre-Platonic Greek thought, causal thinking dominates structuralism—structuralism understood here in our sense of the term—as it seeks to discover etiological causes for the world-process of Becoming. Plato's philosophy of "Forms" rejects this trend of thought, and re-introduces the world of Being and of "formal relationships" as the true reality.[7] But in the system of Aristotle there is a tentative reconciliation of these opposites. On the one hand, Aristotle transforms thought from a theory of concepts into a theory of the actual; and on the other, he reintroduces the knowledge of form as the proper goal of any scientific explanation of the actual world. Aristotle's philosophy thus correlates form and matter, Being and Becoming. Observes Cassirer:

> The peculiarly Aristotelian concept of form-cause originates in this correlativity... . Here the form-principle and the causal principle coincide for both are united in the telic principle.[8]

An extended application of this metaphysical position lies at the basis of Aristotle's poetics. A poetic structure or form is that plot which illustrates the operation of a cause-consequence chain of incidents. The poet is thus a poet (the maker) of his plot, in the causal relationship of the incidents themselves. And poetry is more philosophical than history, for in poetic universality the correlation of the form-principle and the cause-principle is more apparent.

Behind the basis of much of the criticism of the plot of *Paradise Lost*, lies this Aristotelian view of reality as a causal process. Every incident in a plot (as every phenomenon in life) must be causally related to its antecedent and must similarly be connected with what follows. Thus the general tendency in criticism is to seek for a causal antecedent for every incident in the poem, and especially so, for the fall of man. One can see the extreme limit, to which the discussion of the cause of the fall of man in Milton's epic can be carried in John M. Steadman's book *Milton's Epic Characters*.[9]

In literary theory and literary criticism, somehow, this mistaken idea of causal relationship subsists even in our time, while methodo-

---

[7] *Ibid.*; pp. 160 ff.
[8] *Ibid.*, p. 161.
[9] See especially the third part entitled "Logic and the Argument".

logical developments even in the experimental sciences have abandoned the idea of cause long ago. After examining the rejection of the causal concept in the fields of physics, biology, and psychology, Cassirer concludes:

> Over against the concept of cause there emerges the *concept* of structure as the dominant principle. Structure is not understood, it is destroyed when the attempt is made to analyze it into a mere aggregate, a "summation".[10]

Everywhere in modern thought, except in literary theory and criticism, the concepts of "wholeness" and of "structure" have replaced those of causality and process. The actual bases of phenomena cannot be explained by the idea of cause and effect. Logic can explain the bases of thought and of knowledge, but not those of events and of reality.

By the literary myth, then, I mean first, a verbal structure which embodies a peculiar mode of perception (as outlined above), and a view of reality as a structure of relationships. The mythical mode of perception is both objective and subjective in the sense that while it perceives feeling-qualities in the objects perceived, the very object presents itself as wholesome or unwholesome, with an "affective" colouring to man. Thus the idea of good and evil is intrinsic to mythic perception. Here lies, probably, the explanation for the dim intimations of good and evil (not the knowledge of good and evil, but a dim awareness only) in the Adam of *Paradise Lost*, to whom every phenomenon of nature presents itself as good, with the possibility of some distant unidentified evil vaguely hinted at.

Again, the whole of reality is understood and explained by the literary myth in terms of structural relationships. In the mythic theory of man and the world, therefore, the question of the nature of man is ultimately the question of his total relationship to his Maker, to his fellow human beings, and to the world of nature around him. It is only in these senses that I have developed the theory of literary myth, as contradistinguished from the literary plot. In *Paradise Lost*, we have an epic myth, not only in the sense that its story is taken from mythology, but in the more important sense that its narrative is developed according to the mythic view of reality and its mode of perception. The Divine, the human, the

[10] *The Logic of the Humanities*, p. 170.

natural, and the preternatural phenomena in the poem are connected together structurally. Milton illustrates the presence of these forces at the very beginning of Adam's consciousness itself, the presence of an "affective" quality, an element of approval towards all the phenomena of nature. Adam sees all nature around, and the sky and its mysteries above, with joy, wonder, and a blissful sense of participation. The only thing that is to be rejected is the interdicted Tree.

This "feeling-quality" inherent in every perception of Adam leads him to communicate it through the intensely lyrical dialogues with Eve, his partner in the joys of life. We can only understand Adam's pleasurable responsiveness to nature on the basis of the mythic mode of perception. Likewise he responds to Eve instinctively and immediately in terms of conjugal love, and similarly Eve, towards Adam; and both respond in terms of filial love to God. Before the fall, evil is shown (through anticipation) as that which they reject, that to which they react negatively.

Likewise the moral principle of the poem is obedience. Obedience is good because it maintains and sustains the network of relationships between the Divine, the human, and the natural planes of being in the poem. In fact, moral values like freedom and rationality are explained in terms of the ultimate principle for man, namely, his free and loving obedience. In Milton's use of the conceptions of freedom, love, rationality and obedience in *Paradise Lost*, they are interchangeable synonyms. And apart from the principle of love which leads to obedience and which is the relationship between the human and the Divine, and the human and the human, *Paradise Lost* is centred on no other moral category. The structural ordering of the incidents in the epic is determined by the principle of love (or its emotional antithesis, hate). And every incident is correlated to the mythic structure of the poem through the principle of love, or hate. No causal principle operates in determining the disposition of the events, and the development of the action.

We often overlook, due to our misplaced enthusiasm for the faculty psychology of the seventeenth century and its nominal influence on Milton the complex layers of theological and historical perspectives synthesized by him in the epic. To assume that this psychology alone can account for Milton's characterization in the epic is to deny the creative power of Milton and is thus to be insensible to the quality of poetic excellence in *Paradise Lost*.

Coming to the historical dimensions in the epic, we must note the relevance of history to mythology in general which has always been an issue of considerable theoretical interest. In *Paradise Lost* the entire scope of action is within the ambit of historical time. This may sound strange. The usual view that the Divine act of Creation was before the beginning of time, and also that Paradise was in pre-history, finds no support either in Milton's prose or poetry. In his theory, God creates the world in time. He stretches the arguments even further to hint at the possibility that the angels themselves might have been created in time. Paradise is located in time; so also the fall of man. Discussing whether time could have existed before the creation of the material world, and whether the rebellion of the angels could also be within the temporal dimension Milton says in *De Doctrina*:

> ... it seems even probable, that the apostasy which caused the expulsion of so many thousands from heaven took place before the foundations of this world were laid. Certainly there is no sufficient foundation for the common opinion, that motion and time (which is the measure of motion) could not...have existed before this world was made; since Aristotle, who teaches that no ideas of motion and time can be formed except in reference to this world, nevertheless pronounces the world to be eternal.[11]

Temporality and mutability define the historical process. In *Paradise Lost* Adam's nature is perfect but not immutable. Raphael makes this clear to Adam, and to ourselves. Thus the historical process has begun with Paradise. It is created in time. Its human figures are mutable, though perfect. Milton's treatment of time and history has been dismissed without sufficient scrutiny. There is the oft-repeated statement that "Shakespeare lived in a world of time, Milton in a Universe of space". This assertion will not stand critical scrutiny. It can be traced to its original source in David Masson. It is very amusing to see that even so competent a critic and scholar as Majorie Nicolson repeats this with approval. That Milton lived in a universe of space, ignoring the reality of temporal experiences, is an assumption which she makes in all her Milton criticism. It is there in her *Science and Imagination* (p. 56), and in

[11] *The Works*, xv, p. 35.

The Breaking of the Circle (p. 166). In Nicolson's application of the "aesthetics of the infinite" to Milton, she dwells at length on the new idea of the infinite expansiveness of space made available to the seventeenth century through the invention of the telescope.

In fact it has become the fashionable pre-occupation of even the "myth critics" of Milton like Isabel MacCaffrey to comment on the "space intoxication" of Milton. Dealing with the structural patterns in *Paradise Lost* (in Chapter Seven of her book *Paradise Lost as "Myth"*), she says that Milton understates the effects of time, as all poetry based on myth is a "continual struggle to abrogate time".[12] She does not take into account the mythic modes of perceiving time and space. Consequently, in her view, "The special history of *Paradise Lost* is prehistory; the memory evoked is something like racial memory".[13] The mythology of the poem has once again been reduced into a repository of Jungian archetypes.

Indeed, Milton's special literary re-construction of the mythology of the Genesis lies in locating it in time and incorporating into the Biblical myth the idea of mutability, thereby stressing the temporal and historical dimensions of experience. Milton treats the Genesis story not as a *repertoire* of Jungian archetypes, but as history itself, the very beginning, and the very analogue of the historical process. Milton had St. Augustine's example in formulating a theory of history on the basis of the contents of the Genesis.

Let us compare Miltons's use of myth and history in *Paradise Lost* with the use of myths in modern times for developing a philosophy of history. The most useful comparison will be between Milton and a historian who uses the same type of myths as that used by Milton, namely, the "genesis" myths, or the myths which explain the origin of mankind and the growth of the historical processes. We have such an example in Arnold J. Toynbee. Toynbee in *A Study of History* uses the same Biblical Mythology of the Genesis to provide a basis for his interpretation of history.[14] His historical interpretation of the Genesis myth will be a modern analogue for Milton's epic interpretation of the same myth. This fact itself will disprove Waldock's contention that:

A glance at the story of the Fall as it is given in Genesis shows

[12] See pp. 46 ff.
[13] *Paradise Lost as "Myth"*, p. 42.
[14] See especially Volume I, pp. 272-338.

that it is linked with difficulties of the gravest order.... The story in the Genesis was like a stretch of film minutely flawed. Milton's plan was to take this and project it on an enormous canvas. Must he not (we wonder sometimes) have foreseen the effect of the tremendous enlargement : that every slight imperfection would show that every rift would become a gulf.[15]

The procedural error in Waldock's criticism of *Paradise Lost* lies in rigidly and artificially distinguishing between the techniques of the narrative in myths and in modern fiction, and in excluding from myths their concern with reality. He seems to argue that the myths are " mythological " and that they have no concern with the problems of human relationship and conduct.

Toynbee has shown the similarity, on the other hand, between the narrative techniques in myths and modern fiction. The only difference is the greater concern of the myth with reality, and the wider scope of its treatment of the same. The themes of the ancient etiological myths comprehend not only personal human relationships, but in addition include a variety of questions on collective relationships, and on the history and the final destiny of man. The literary fiction of modern times is much more restricted in scope and concerns; it deals with inter-personal and intra-personal relationships. And whenever fiction, properly so defined, exceeds the scope of these, it becomes, whether novel or drama, epic in dimensions, and thereby indirectly creates its own myth. Apart from this, according to Toynbee, the narrative techniques and the character of the verbal structures in both modern fiction and ancient mythology are essentially the same.

Toynbee explains his theory of literary fiction (whether ancient mythology or modern fiction) as follows. Literary fiction, or that which is the product of the creative imagination, does not "present fictions", in the sense of "complete fictions, and nothing but fictions regarding the personal relations of human beings. Besides fictions they present facts and laws".[16] A literary fiction or "myth" is both fact and fiction at the same time; the distinction between fact and fiction is undrawn. The fiction supplements the facts through interpreting them. In the words of Toynbee:

[15]Waldock, *op. cit.*, pp. 18-19.
[16]*A Study of History*, I, 448.

When we call a piece a 'work of ficition', we mean no more than that the characters could not be identified with any persons who have lived in the flesh, nor the incidents and scenes with any events or situations that have actually occurred. In fact, we mean that this work has fictitious personal foreground; and if we do not mention that the background is composed of authentic social facts, this is simply because this seems so self-evident that we take it for granted.[17]

Literary fiction as the record of authentic social facts is a truer interpretation of human nature than the social sciences, and also the literary forms cannot be interpreted in terms of sociological or anthropological factors. Toynbee is emphatic in stating that history too must look to techniques of fictional analyses for its ground and source of meaning. And history as well as modern literary forms has its origin in mythology. He says:

...The Drama and the Novel grew out of Mythology, which is like-wise the source of 'History' and ... in Mythology the distinction between facts and fiction is left undrawn.... The Hellenic Drama and Hellenic History had a common literary parent in the Homeric Epic, which was the literary vehicle of the Hellenic Mythology; and when we examine the plots of the earliest Greek plays, we find that they are taken from this or that incident or situation in the Epic Cycle. Similarly, the 'Mystery Plays' in which our Western Drama first emerged took their plots from the Gospels and from the legends of Christ and the Saints, which may be regarded as the epic cycle in the background of our Western History. Thus, in Greek tragedies and in Western 'Mystery Plays' alike, the plots originally belonged to a realm in which the question 'Is this fact or fiction?' did not arise....[18]

If we transfer this conception wholly to Milton's epic, there can never be a more complete explanation of Milton's technique of combining myth and history through a poetic conception of the structure of reality. The story of the Genesis had, for Milton's imagination, the potentialities of being developed into a literary

[17] *Ibid.*, p. 449.
[18] *Ibid.*, pp. 448-9.

myth in which fact and fiction cohere, and in which the known facts of life can project the yet unknown truths of history. Let us look more closely into the theories of the myth, and the connection which Toynbee establishes between the "genesis" myths and history, and try to see if these can partly elucidate the themes and the narrative technique of *Paradise Lost*.

CHAPTER TEN

THE "GENESIS" MYTHS AND HISTORY ARNOLD J. TOYNBEE ON THE GENESIS MYTHS

A VARIETY OF approaches to myths in general has brought out their psychological, anthropological, and philosophic contents. A careful study of these contents has thrown much light on many aspects of poetic themes. Literary criticism and interpretation have both benefited through the application of conceptual developments in our modern theories of the myths. But the historical contents of the myths and their historical analysis have to be similarly correlated to the task of interpretation and criticism in literature. An historian's analysis of the myths has as much literary validity as those of the psychologist and the anthropologist. Indeed, in some types of poetry like the epic, and historical drama and the novel in which not only the historical contents but more importantly the historical dimension of human experience provides the framework of action, the historical implications of the myths are more relevant and useful.

Where man's subjective experiences inspire poetry, the psychoanalytical contents of the myth provide useful tools for analyses. But when poetry is concerned with man's collective, objective experiences through time, and with the interconnection between the past and the present, and the directions of the future, then the points of contact between myth and history acquire poetical relevance.

If myth is not history in the proper sense, neither is it pre-history. But the myths embody patterns of events, and bear traces of energies which are later actualized in the march of human history; and in these lie the connection between myth and history. The philosopher of history and the historian of human institutions, cultures, and civilizations, must deal not with particulars, but through the particulars with the universal like the poet (of Aristotle). Here is where the mythical imagination—in our sense of the term— and the poetical imagination co-operate, and often coalesce into one.

To see how one group of myths which deal with the origin of mankind has been treated from the historian's standpoint, we must turn to Arnold J. Toynbee. Trying to trace the patterns of evolution and dissolution of civilizations and the energies which direct their growth and decay, Toynbee conceives of these factors in terms of the action of challenge and response between two superhuman personalities. In his own words, "the causes of geneses of civilizations is not simple but multiple, it is not an entity but a relation."[1]

We have the choice of conceiving this relation either as an interaction between two inhuman factors or as an "encounter between two superhuman personalities". And, an encounter between two super-human personalities and the influence of this conflict on man's history and destiny is the plot of a group of myths which I have called the genesis myths. This central content is present in many myths ranging from the Sinic stories of Yin and Yang, in the Far East; the Syriac and the Hebrew myths of Yahweh and Satan, and their encounter; in the Greeks myths of Titanomachia; and in the teachings of the philosopher Empedocles in whose philosophy the conflicting personalities are personifications of Love and Hate. In the Book of Job, in the Bible Story of Genesis, in the Yin and Yang Story, in Goethe's *Faust*, in Euripides's *Hippolytus*, and in Milton's *Paradise Lost*, and *Paradise Regained*, the variations of these central myths constitute the theme.

It is interesting to see how Toynbee demonstrates the presence of two such abstractions in scientific thought, though rendered impersonal, which even astronomers and scientists cannot escape while formulating their theories of the origin of the world. Instead of Yahweh and Serpent, or Yin and Yang, we have a conflict between a primeval cloud, and cloud; a star, and a star in the inconceivable backward stretch of time. The idea of the conflict is there. Instead of personalities, we have clouds of matter, or vapour, or energy concentrations, or stars.

After searching for that unknown factor which can account for the growth of civilization, the cyclic progress of mankind from the static condition, through a dynamic state, to a staticity again, and after rejecting race, milieu, and environment, Toynbee says:

if your unknown quantity is neither Race nor Environment,

[1] *A Study of History*, p. 271.

neither God nor the Devil, it cannot be a simple quantity but must be a product of two: some interaction between Environment and Race, some encounter between the Devil and God. That is the plot of the Book of Job and the plot of Goethe's *Faust*. Is it, perhaps, the plot of Life and the plot of History?[2]

This encounter between the Devil and God, Milton has made "the plot of life and the plot of history" in *Paradise Lost*. This itself is a valid reason for instituting a comparison between the use of the same theme in a poem of the seventeenth century, and a philosophy of history of the Modern Age. Apart from this fact there is the usual criticism against Milton's handling of the story of the fall which we must look into. And those who are unable to see and respond to the links which Milton establishes among the various incidents in the plot of his epic attribute these "failures" to the fact that Milton selected a myth, restricted in scope and content; a sectarian myth suitable to a particular religious world view; a myth which, through want of universality, could not embody universal human feelings. Being pre-scientific and simplicistic, it could not embody the complexities of life. This choice of the poetic theme itself, they say, is a direct indication of Milton's defective poetic imagination.

This charge loses its weight when we see that a philosopher and historian of the Twentieth Century, who has had the benefit of the achievements of three centuries of science and "liberation", rejects these very achievements as inadequate to comprehend life's phenomena and falls back on the contents of the same mythology as that of Milton's poem.

The validity of my own critical procedure here is due to yet another reason. When the structural treatment of a theme becomes critically intractable, it is useful to set it beside a handling of the same theme in another medium for comparison and contrast. One of my main contentions is that the myth of *Paradise Lost* has to be correlated to its historical vision, and in Toynbee's correlation of myth and history we have a modern analogue for what Milton did in his poetry. Although Toynbee uses the Genesis myth for elucidating historical phenomena, his method of interpreting historical data combines the achievements of the sciences with those of creative literature. Thus in comparing Milton's handling of the

[2] *Ibid.*, Vol. I, pp. 270-1.

same mythic material with Toynbee's, we are comparing the operations of a pre-scientific poetic imagination with those of a modern, scientific, and critical intelligence, on human nature. In the one we have theological commitments and poetic subjectivity, in the other intellectual detachment and historical objectivity. But strangely enough, we will find that their conclusions mutually support, and mutually elucidate each other. I shall briefly set forth Toynbee's theory of the genesis myth here, quoting him profusely.

In Toynbee's system of historical thought which he expounds in his monumental work *A Study of History*, history in the popular sense is a study of the social phenomena of civilizations.[3] The subject of history is the study of institutional relations and, since myth and creativities deal with personal relations, in both there is a procedural similarity. History and creative writings and myth and literature, all study human relations, one impersonal, the other personal. Societies themselves are simply institutions of the highest order.[4] The study of societies and the study of institutional relations are one and the same thing.[5] And social institutions themselves are social mechanisms created to maintain the social relations of human beings.[6] While the social relations of human beings are impersonal, in the sense of extending "beyond the furthest possible range of personal contacts", they have yet a reality of their own, as personal relations. Many examples will show, in his view, that

> ...while institutional relations are truly impersonal they are in no sense unreal. Indeed, they are the elements in human life in virtue of which we have accepted the definition of Man as being a social animal.[7]

History therefore becomes the study of impersonal, social relations. True, according to Toynbee, the whole reality of human consciousness cannot be defined in terms of social relations, and not even by personal relations, for there are intense individual experiences like inspiration, genius, mystical intuitions, which are not "relationships." Yet, even these individual experiences become

[3]*Ibid.*, Vol. I, p. 442.
[4]*Ibid.*, p. 455.
[5]*Ibid.*
[6]*Ibid.*, p. 454.
[7]*Ibid.*, p. 454 n.

relevant and meaningful to mankind through their "potent social effect".⁸ These then, are the subject-matter of history. Among the three techniques usually employed to view the data of history (i.e. the phenomena of life) the objective, analytical method of the empirical sciences, the comparative method of the normative social sciences, and the technique of artistic creation and expression, Toynbee considers the technique of literary creation the most useful one for historical investigation; literature deals with personal human relations; history deals with impersonal human relations, though these are only impersonal in the sense of being institutional. So the techniques used in creative literature can be fruitfully employed in throwing light on the genesis of civilizations. For

> ... 'History' grew out of Mythology, a primitive intuitive form of apprehension in which the Drama and the Novel likewise took their origin. In Mythology, the distinction between facts and fictions is left undrawn; and while 'History' has differentiated itself from Mythology by making an effort to extract the facts, it has never succeeded in dispensing with fictitious elements altogether.⁹

Accordingly one must have recourse to mythology to find the genesis of the historical phenomena of human life. The historian can communicate his insight only

> by the technique called 'fiction' which our dramatists and novelists employ in our time in order to communicate to their fellowmen their thoughts and feelings about the personal relations of human beings—about those human lives and deaths, those personal successes and failures, those individual hopes and fears, which have repeated themselves, since Mankind became human, until their name is legion.¹⁰

The application of literary techniques to historical processes discovers that their origins lie in the mutation of primitive societies into civilizations. And this mutation consists in the "transition from a static condition to a dynamic activity".¹¹ This transition

---
⁸*Ibid.*
⁹*Ibid.*, p. 442.
¹⁰*Ibid.*, p. 464.
¹¹*Ibid.*, p. 195.

accounts for the genesis of civilizations. But what accounts for this transition itself? Race and Milieu? Or natural environment and human response? A detailed examination of all the evidences in their favour leads to their rejection by Toynbee.[12] And then he develops his historical concept of "Challenge-and-Response,"[13] which in various mythologies embodies the idea of a "rhythm" in the life of mankind, the ebb and flow of a directing energy, or a rhythm which controls the alternate ebb and flow of two forces which are complementary to one another and at the same time antithetical. The presence of this rhythm is considered as something fundamental in the universe, and we come upon this alternate ebb and flow of a simultaneously complementary and antithetical energy whether we approach human phenomenon through anthropology or psychology, sociology or history, ancient mythology or modern science. Quoting from the Fragments (No. 20) of Empedocles, Toynbee calls our attention to "an integrating force which he (Empedocles) calls 'Love' and a disintegrating force which he calls 'Hate' ".[14]

The two alternating forces or phases in the rhythm of the Universe which Empedocles calls Love and Hate are also present in all the mythologies of the world.[15] The cause of the genesis of civilization is "not simple but multiple; it is not an entity but a relation", a conflicting relation which generates the rhythm of love and hate.

> We have the choice of conceiving this relation either as an interaction between two inhuman forces—like the petrol and the air which interact in the engine of a motor car—or an encounter between two super-human personalities.[16]

The second of these conceptions is a surer foundation for explaining the world processes. This super-human encounter, this prehistoric conflict generates the tensions in history and accounts for civilizational differentiations. Such an encounter is a unique event. Although modern scientific imagination will be inclined to reject the concept of a unique personal conflict, modern astronomy

[12]*Ibid.*, pp. 207-71.
[13]*Ibid.*, pp. 271 ff.
[14]*Ibid.*, p. 200.
[15]*Ibid.*, p. 201.
[16]*Ibid.*

frequently uses the idea of a collision between two stellar bodies to account for the beginning of the cosmic systems and, as Toynbee argues, given the immensity of the cosmos, on the basis of mathematical probability, the possibility of such a stellar conflict can be considered as unique as the mythical conception of a unique personal conflict. The idea of the unique primeval conflict is there both in science, and mythology, but mythology only personalizes this conflict and, in so doing, provides the authentic basis for an historical explanation of human phenomena. Toynbee's own lucid exposition of the theme of Love-Hate antithesis, "the Action of Challenge-and-Response", between two super-human personalities, the theme of a super-human conflict as a fundamental theme in world history and mythology, had better be quoted in his own words :

…An encounter between two super-human personalities is the plot of some of the greatest stories and dramas that the human imagination has conceived. An encounter between Yahweh and the Serpent in the plot of the story of the Fall of Man in the Book of Genesis; a second encounter between the same antagonists…is the plot of the New Testament which tells the story of the Redemption; an encounter between the Lord and Satan in the plot of the Book of Job; an encounter between Gods and Demons in the plot of the Scandinavian *Voluspa*; an encounter between Artemis and Aphrodite in the plot of Euripides, Hippolytus.[17]

The two general features of such an encounter are its uniqueness and the "consequences are…vast in proportion to the vastness of the breach which it makes in the customary course of Nature."[18] In all these stories, the consequences which are felt on the Earth of this unusual encounter in Heaven are tremendous.

The single ordeals of Job and Faust represent in the intuitive language of fiction the infinitely multiple ordeal of Man; and, in the language of theology, the same vast consequence is represented as following from the super-human encounters that are portrayed in the Book of Genesis and in the New Testament. The expulsion of Adam and Eve from the Garden of Eden, which

[17]*Ibid.*, pp. 271-2.
[18]*Ibid.*, p. 244.

follows from the encounter between Yahweh and the Serpent, is nothing less than the Fall of Man, the passion of Christ in the New Testament is nothing less than Man's Redemption.[19]

In the Bible the uniqueness of the event is of the essence of the story, and this uniqueness has been a stumbling block to the scientific intellect ever since the geo-centric theory of the world was impugned. And

> Milton, who was acquainted with, and probably convinced by the heliocentric system of Copernicus, avoided this stumbling block by deliberately following the geo-metric system of Ptolemy when he set the stage for *Paradise Lost*.[20]

In the language of mythology the impulse or motive which accounts for the transition from a state of ideal perfection to that of historical actuality comes from the intrusion of the Devil into the universe of God. According to Toynbee, this event can be best described in these mythological images without those contradictions that arise when the statement is translated into logical terms.

In the logical system, if God's universe is perfect, there cannot be a Devil outside it, while, if the Devil exists, the perfection which he comes to spoil must have been incomplete already through the very fact of his existence.[21]

> This logical contradiction which cannot logically be resolved is intuitively transcended in the imagery of the poet and the prophet, who give glory to God yet take it for granted that he is subject to two crucial limitations.
> The first limitation is that, in the perfection of what he has created already, He cannot find an opportunity for further creative activity.... The second limitation upon God's power is that when the opportunity for fresh creation is offered to Him from outside, He cannot but take it. When the Devil challenges Him, He cannot refuse to take up the challenge....This limitation is illustrated in the Parable of the Tares.
> 'So the servants of the householder came and said unto him:

[19] *Ibid.*, p. 274.
[20] *Ibid.*
[21] *Ibid.*, p. 279.

"Sir, didst thou not sow good seed in thy field? From whence, then, hath it tares?", He said unto them: "An enemy hath done this". The servants said unto him: "Wilt thou then that we go and gather them up?" But he said: Nay; lest, while ye gather all the tares, you root up also the wheat with them. Let both grow together until the harvest." (Matthew, xiii, 27-30).[22]

Toynbee reasons that according to the poetic imaginations and prophetic intuitions

> God is bound to accept the predicament thrust upon Him by the Devil because He can only refuse at the price of renouncing His own purposes and undoing His own work—in fact at the price of denying His own nature and ceasing to be God, which is either an impossibility or another story.
> If God is thus not omnipotent in logical terms, is He still mythologically invincible? If He is bound to take up the Devil's challenge, is He equally bound to win the ensuing battle?[23]

In some versions of the mythical conflict between God and Devil, the combat which follows the compulsory acceptance by God of the Devil's challenge takes the form of a "wager which the Devil is apparently bound to lose".[24]

The classic works of art in which this Wager-motif is worked out are the Book of Job and Goethe's *Faust*. Toynbee comments on the nature of the Wager, and the outcome of the conflict.

> In both *Job* and *Faust* the Wager is won by God; and again, in the New Testament, the same ending is given, through the revelation of a second encounter between the same pair of antagonists, to the combat between Yahweh and the Serpent... .Moreover in *Job* and *Faust* and the New Testament alike it is suggested, or even declared outright, that the wager cannot be won by the Devil; that the Devil, in meddling with God's work cannot frustrate but can only serve the purpose of God, who remains master of the situations all the time and gives the Devil

[22] *Ibid.*, pp. 278-80.
[23] *Ibid.*, pp. 279-80.
[24] *Ibid.*, p. 280.

rope for the Devil to hang himself....²⁵

If it is declared outright that God is going to win the wager, has the Devil been cheated? Did God accept a wager, which he knew all the time that He could not lose? If this were true the whole "God-Devil" encounter would be a sham, and could not have produced those vast transitions in human history. One possible explanation suggested by Toynbee is that

> the wager which the Devil offers, and which God accepts, covers not the whole of God's creation but only a part. The part, not the whole, is at stake; yet the chances and changes to which the part is thus exposed cannot possibly leave the whole unaffected.
> ... In the language of Mythology when one of Gods's creatures is tempted by the Devil, God Himself is given an opportunity to recreate the World.... When once the divine equilibrium has been upset by the Satanic instability, the Devil has shot his bolt; and the restoration of equilibrium on a new plan, in which God's purpose is fulfilled lies wholly within God's power. In this act the sole permanent and significant result of the transaction between God and the Devil, 'no demon is' or can be, 'at work'.²⁶

Thus the Devil is bound to lose the wager not because he has been cheated by God, but because the Devil has overreached himself. Through the malicious satisfaction of forcing God's hand the Devil has played into God's own hands, for although he knew that God neither would nor could refuse the offer of the wager if made to him, he did not observe that God was eagerly hoping that the offer would be made. In the Devil's malicious jubilation at obtaining an opportunity to ruin God's choicest creature or creatures, the Devil did not and could not foresee that through his offer he was giving God an opportunity to renew the whole work of creation, an opportunity for which God was waiting. "And so God's purpose is fulfilled through the Devil's instrumentality and in the Devil's despite."²⁷

The object of the wager is always God's creature. The crisis of

---
²⁵*Ibid.*, pp. 282-3.
²⁶*Ibid.*, p. 284.
²⁷*Ibid.*, p. 285.

the plot turns upon the role of God's creature, a Job, an Adam, or a Faust. This chosen vessel, the creation of God, is their common field of action, the arena in which they do battle. He plays a multiple role.

He is also the combatant as well as the arena and the dramatic personnel as well as the stage. Created by God and abandoned to the Devil he is seen, in the prophet's vision, to be an incarnation of both his Maker and his Tempter, while, in the psychologist's analysis, God and the Devil alike are reduced to conflicting psychic forces in his soul—forces which have no independent existence apart from the symbolic language of Mythology.[28]

In every literary presentation of this conflict, suffering is the keynote of the human protagonist's part. Suffering consists of a series of stages which the sufferer has to pass through in order to serve God's purpose.

Toynbee's analysis of the conflict between God and the Devil in the arena of man, otherwise called the temptation of man, and the comparative study of the same phenomena in various similar genesis myths, elucidates many aspects of the narrative in Milton's Epic. The God-Satan encounter staged in the heart of man presents itself as an ordeal which the protagonist has to carry out. As in Adam's case, when assaulted with the temptation, he has to take energetic action to resist it. In Toynbee's words:

> Objectively, the ordeal consists of a series of stages which the sufferer has to pass through in order to serve God's purpose. In the first place, the human protagonist in the drama takes action— in reaction to an assault from the tempter—which sets up a change from passivity to activity, from rest to motion, from calm to storm, from harmony to discord....The action may be either dynamically base, as when the Ancient Mariner shoots the Albatros ...or dynamically sublime as when Jesus, in the temptation in the wilderness which immediately follows his baptism in Jordan, rejects the traditional Jewish role of the Messiah who was to raise the Chosen people to dominion in this world by the sword. The essence of the act is not its moral character but its dynamic effect.[29]

[28] *Ibid.*, pp. 285-6.
[29] *Ibid.*, pp. 277-88.

The story of the Fall of Man in Genesis is analysed in historical terms, by Toynbee as follows :

> In the story of the Fall in the Book of Genesis, the dynamic act is Eve's eating of the fruit of the Tree of Knowledge at the serpent's prompting ; and here the application of the myth to the genesis of civilization is direct. The picture of Adam and Eve in the Garden of Eden is a reminiscence of (the ideal state of rest) to which Primitive Man attained, in 'the food-gathering phase' of economy, after he had established his ascendancy over all the rest of the flora and fauna of the Earth—the state which is remembered in the Hellenic Mythology as "the Times of Cronos", the Fall in response to the temptations to taste the fruit of the Tree of the Knowledge of Good and Evil, symbolizes the acceptance of a challenge to abandon the achieved integration and to venture upon a fresh differentiation out of which another integration may—or may not—arise. The expulsion from the Garden into an unfriendly outer world in which the Woman must bring forth children in sorrow and the Man must eat bread in sweat of his face, is the ordeal which the acceptance of the serpent's challenge has entailed. The sexual intercourse between Adam and Eve, which follows, is an act of social creation. It bears fruit in the birth of two sons who impersonate two nascent civilizations : Abel the keeper of sheep and Cain the tiller of the ground.
> ...The second stage in the human protagonists ordeal is the crisis. He realizes that his dynamic act, which has re-liberated the creative power of his Master and Maker, has set his own feet on a course which is leading him to suffering and death. In an agony of disillusionment and horror, he rebels against the fate, which by his own act, he has brought upon himself for God's gain. The crisis is resolved when he resigns himself consciously to be the instrument of God's will, the tool in God's hand; and this activity through passivity, this victory through defeat, brings on another cosmic change. Just as the dynamic act in the first phase of the ordeal shook the Universe out of calm into storm, so the act of resignation in the second phase reverses the rhythm of the Universe—guiding it now from motion towards rest, from storm towards calm from, discord towards harmony....[30]

[30] *Ibid.*, pp. 290-1.

THE "GENESIS" MYTHS AND HISTORY

Our search for the poetic understanding of man must begin, not with the concept of the nature of man, for as Ortega Y. Gasset said "Man has no nature, What he has is...history."[31] Probably this view of the interconnection between myth and history can throw some light on the structure and the theme of *Paradise Lost*, and on the correlation between epic incidents and epic characterization.

---

[31] "History as a System", in *Philosophy and History, Essays presented to Ernst Cassirer*, p. 293, quoted by Cassirer in *An Essay on Man*, p. 172.

CHAPTER ELEVEN

STRUCTURE AND THEME IN *PARADISE LOST*

THE CIRCUMAMBIENT MYTH of *Paradise Lost* is based on the Bible stories of the rebellion and rout of Satan, the creation of the world and man, and man's apostasy. Its intractability can impose a strain on the creative freedom of the poet in determining the combination of incidents in the structure of the poem. Milton overcomes this restrictive quality of his myth by reconstructing it in such a manner as to subordinate the elements of the story to its theoretical elements. Every myth, as Cassirer says, "combines a theoretical element and an element of artistic creation".[1]

Every myth has an element of truth and an element of fiction too; and a poem based on the myth must transform these into the truth of fiction. In this process of transformation, the myth itself is re-created as the theme of the poem. In Milton's myth, the theoretical element is the genesis and the progress of history, and the poetic theme illustrates the dynamisms which pattern the historical movements, and the energies which control their rhythms.

These energies are the creative principle of love, and the destructive principle of hate. Briefly, in one phrase, we can state the essential theme of *Paradise Lost* as the sustained opposition between love and hate. God responds to the destructive challenge of Satan with the creative expression of love. In this larger theme of "love-versus-hate" antithesis are subsumed all the other themes of *Paradise Lost*.

The structure of the incidents in the narrative is determined by the principle of contrast. The general mythical framework is the myth of the conflict between two Superhuman Personalities, in its Biblical form. Milton has combined two traditional elements in this historical myth, the story of the God-Devil encounter, and the story of the challenge and response, through an indirect agent. The former theme is the direct physical conflict of the Celestial

[1] *An Essay on Man*, p. 75.

Battle, and the latter is Satan's challenge of God, indirectly through God's own creature, man. This theme is best illustrated in *Job*. The "challenge-and-response" theme is the sequel to this first theme of the Divine-Demonic conflict, and arises out of it, and thus both are complementary to each other.

In *Paradise Lost*, the Divine-Demonic encounter is not the principal event, and it lies outside its framework of action, in the sense that it is a secondary narration within the primary narrative of the poem. It is not its structural incident, but only its antecedent. Raphael's story of the war in Heaven establishes the poem's antecedents. The initial epic incident is the expulsion of Satan from Heaven, the physical fall of the rebel angel and his crew. The initiating incident begins at

> What time his Pride
> Had cast him out from Heav'n, with all his Host....
>
> (i. 36-38)

The physical fall of Satan follows the spiritual fall earlier, and is a consequence of it.

> Him the Almighty Power
> Hurl'd headlong flaming from the Ethereal Sky
> With hideous ruin and combustion down
> To bottomless perdition.
>
> (i. 44-47)

This image of the physical fall is again repeated in terms of another fall taken from classical mythology, the fall of Mulciber.

> Men call'd him *Mulciber*, and how he fell
> From Heav'n, they fabl'd, thrown by angry *Jove*
> Sheer o'er the Crystal Battlements: from Morn
> To Noon he fell, from Noon to dewy Eve,
> A Summer's day; and with the setting Sun
> Dropt from the Zenith like a falling Star.
>
> (i. 740-745)

The fall of Satan as the first initiating incident of the poem anticipates its epic crisis, the fall of man. Satan's expulsion from

Heaven is more graphically presented in Book Six (lines 855 to 877). This expulsion is the occasion for two significant developments, the creation of the world, and the subsequent intrusion of evil into this world created by God as perfect.

The poetic postulate that along with an Omnipotent and Omnipresent God, there can also co-exist a Devil who can challenge Him, and give battle, is a logical contradiction and, to reason, it is an offence. But the poetical and mythical imagination makes use of this very contradiction for its theme. As Toynbee has shown, in all the genesis myths, the Deity, though all-powerful and all-knowing, is subject to three crucial limitations which poetic imagination has no difficulty in conceiving along with God's omnipotence and omnipresence. These limitations are the following:

In the first place, when the Devil challenges God, either for Battle or for Wager, God cannot but accept the challenge. For, a refusal to accept either challenge would be inconsistent with God's nature. Second, God cannot begin the work of creation unless an opportunity offers itself. Third, and when the occasion for creation arises, God cannot but welcome the opportunity for creation.

Implicit in the myth is yet another assumption, almost a corollary to those above, that God cannot destroy anything He has created. In all these numerous myths which deal with the origin of mankind, God's Being is so conceived that if any of these premises is denied, then God ceases to be omnipotent, omnipresent, and omniscient. In the *Christian Doctrine*, Milton attempts a logical proof why God cannot annihilate any created thing; for all things are not only *from* God, but *of* God. Thus no created thing can be annihilated, because

> God is neither willing, nor, properly speaking, able to annihilate anything altogether. He is not "willing, because he does everything with a view to some end"; but nothing can be the end neither of God, nor of anything whatever.... Again, God is not able to annihilate anything altogether, because by creating nothing he would create and not create at the same time, which involves a contradiction.[2]

So God could not have destroyed Satan and the rebel angels. The Celestial War, then instead of being an occasion for destruction, is

[2] *The works,* xv, p. 27.

an opportunity for fresh creation. Adam asks Raphael in Book Seven:

> what cause
> Mov'd the Creator in his holy Rest
> Through all Eternity so late to build
> In *Chaos*, and the work begun, how soon
> Absolv'd, if unforbid thou mayst unfold
> What wee, not to explore the secrets ask
> Of his Eternal Empire, but the more
> To magnify his works, the more we know.
>
> (vii. 90-97)

Raphael traces the occurrence of the idea of creation in God's mind directly to the revolt, the rout and the final expulsion of Satan from Heaven, in lines 131 to 174. Immediately after this follows the long account of creation covering the rest of Book Seven, and the whole of Book Eight.

The principle of structural contrasts begins to operate from this moment, when the thought of creation occurred to God, immediately after Satan's fall into Hell. The creation of man is conceived when

> th' Omnipotent
> Eternal Father from his Throne beheld
> Thir multitude, and to his Son thus spake.
>
> (vii. 136-138)

What God the Father spoke was that He

> in a moment will create
> Another World, out of one man a Race
> Of men innumerable....
>
> (vii. 154-156)

This is that deliberation of the Deity before creation of which Milton speaks in *De Doctrina Christiana*.

Previously, however, to the creation of man, as to intimate the superior importance of the work, the Deity speaks like to a man deliberating....³

Although the greater part of the angels has remained faithful, Satan should not be allowed to feel that he has succeeded in dispeopling Heaven even partially. So the creation is designed both to replenish Heaven, and to humiliate Satan further:

> But lest his heart exalt him in the harm
> Already done, to have dispeopl'd Heav'n
> My damage fondly deem'd I can repair
> That detriment, if such it be to lose
> Self-lost, and in a moment will create
> Another world, out of one man a Race
> Of men innumerable, there to dwell,
> Not here, till by degrees of merit rais'd
> They open to themselves at length the way
> Up hither, under long obedience tr'd,
> And Earth be chang'd to Heav'n, and Heav'n to Earth,
> One Kingdom, Joy and Union without end.
>
> (vii. 150-161)

This speech creates the entire structural framework of epic action for the poem, and the Divine scheme for the world process. Originating in God, this process must return to Him, but only after man has been "under long obedience tried". Structurally, the crucial theme of temptation too has already been anticipated by this speech.

The immediate consequence of the God-Devil encounter, which is not ended with the overthrow of Satan, leads to the second theme of the Devil's challenge of God, and God's creative response to it. The second indirect encounter between them is only another phase of the same old conflict. With this we turn to Milton's commencement of the epic in *media res*:

> The First Book proposes, first in brief, the whole subject, *Man's disobedience, and the loss thereupon of Paradise wherein he was plac't*: Then touches *the prime cause of his fall, the Serpent*, or rather Satan *in the Serpent*.... Which action past over, the Poem hastes into the midst of things....

³ *The Works*, xv, p. 37.

But the first conflict has generated the energies of movements, and the forces which pulse throughout the epic plot. These are the energies, or the forces of love and hate. The end of the first epic battle has not been ultimately conclusive, in the sense that Satan has not been annihilated utterly. His defeat has only served the purpose of releasing a new power in the world, the power of hate, which tests its strength against the antithetical force of Love, personified in God. From now on, the epic events move forward on the crest of the waves set up by the antithesis between love and hate. The "love-hate" antithesis is not only a recurrent motif in the poem, but it is the central poetic theme. The first crisis in the long "God-Satan" encounter, the Celestial Battle, besides defining the mythical cause of which the history of the world is the consequence, also releases the dynamic forces which determine the shape of history, forces which provide the mythical connection between events, and explain the nature of its crisis in the fall of man. The rhythms of epic movements are the rhythms of the ebb and flow of love and hate.

With this "love-hate" antithesis begins the second phase of the Super-Human Encounter, Satan's indirect challenge of God through His creature, and this is the specific mythological theme of *Paradise Lost*. In some versions of this story, Satan lays a wager on man against God. In *Job*, and Goethe's *Faust*, the wager is won by God. In the New Testament, the same victory of God over Satan is promised in the revelation of a second conflict between God the Son and Satan. In Milton's story, although Satan does not lay a wager explicitly against God, the same idea is present in the uncertainty of the final outcome of the challenge. Satan's designs on man are known to God, and God has foreknowledge of the fall. But foreknowledge does not make the fall inevitable or necessary. It still remains in the possibility of contingency. This uncertainty of the outcome of the challenge is explicit in all the utterances of Satan in Books One and Two. Besides, in spite of His foreknowledge, God takes every precaution to prevent it, especially by sending a Celestial Instructor to Adam.

Within the mythic narrative of the poem, we have only the promise of God's final victory over Satan, and not the victory itself. God is aware that He is going to lose the challenge temporarily. God foresees the outcome of the challenge in Book Three.

> For Man will heark'n to his glozing lies,
> And easily transgress the sole Command,
> Sole pledge of his obedience: So will fall
> Hee and his faithless Progeny....
>
> (iii. 93-96)

God repeats His foreknowledge of the fall again in Book Ten soon after the news of the fall is reported in Heaven.

>   be not dismay'd
> Nor troubl'd at these tidings from the Earth,
> Which your sincerest care could not prevent,
> Foretold so lately what would come to pass,
> When first this Tempter cross'd the Gulf from Hell.
> I told ye then he should prevail and speed
> On his bad Errand, Man should be seduc't
> And flatter'd out of all, believing lies
> Against his Maker.
>
> (x. 35-43)

If God then accepts this challenge which He knows He is going to lose, it is only because this is an opportunity for God to re-create the world. As Toynbee analyses the paradox of God's temporary loss of the wager, and his real and final victory:

> In the language of Mythology, when one of God's creatures is tempted by the Devil, God Himself is thereby given the opportunity to recreate the World.... When once the divine equilibrium has been upset by the Satanic instability, the Devil has shot his bolt; and the restoration of the equilibrium on a new plan, in which God's purpose is fulfilled, is wholly whithin God's power. In this act of creation, which is the sole permanent and significant result of the transaction between God and the Devil, 'no demon is,' or can be 'at work'.[4]

Thus, in the long run:

> The Devil is bound to lose the wager, not because he has been cheated by God, but because he has overreached himself.... In

[4] *A Study of History*, I, p. 284.

his jubilation at obtaining an opportunity to ruin one of God's choicest creatures, the Devil did not foresee that he would be giving God Himself an opportunity to renew the whole work of creation. And so God's purpose is fulfilled through the Devil's instrumentality and the Devil's despite.[5]

In Milton's poem, this motif of God recreating the world, after and through Satan's challenge is repeated in all important points of the narrative. Immediately after the first full description of Satan in Book One (lines 191-207) its thematic importance is introduced.

> So stretcht out huge in length the Arch-fiend lay
> Chain'd on the burning Lake, nor ever thence
> Had ris'n or heav'd his head, but that the will
> And high permission of all-ruling Heaven
> Left him at large to his own dark designs,
> That with reiterated crimes he might
> Heap on himself damnation, while he sought
> Evil to others, and enrag'd might see
> How all his malice serv'd but to bring forth
> Infinite goodness, grace and mercy shown
> On Man by him Seduc't....
>
> (i. 209-219)

The "challenge-and-response" theme operates on the level of the transformation of continuous destruction into continuous re-creation. The energy of destruction is confronted and overcome at every level by the energy of creation and re-creation. Speaking in terms of poetic conceptions, this is Milton's "great argument,"—the assertion of the Eternal Providence, and justification of the ways of God to men.

That God has to be challenged indirectly through His Creation is the initial decision which sets the epic action into movement. So momentous a decision, arising out of insurmountable despair, is arrived at by the Infernal Peers through the space of two Books of the epic. In the first speech of Satan to the assembly of the fallen angels in Book One (lines 623-662), Satan anticipates the exploration of new fields and areas of conflict.

[5] *Ibid.* I, pp. 284-5.

He says:

> our better part remains
> To work in close design, by fraud or guile....
> Space may produce new Worlds; whereof so rife
> There went a fame in Heav'n that he ere long
> Intended to create, and therein plant
> A generation, whom his choice regard
> Should favor equal to the Sons of Heaven:
> Thither, if but to pry, shall be perhaps
> Our first eruption....
>
> (i. 645-656)

This anticipation of a new creation as simultaneously the field and object of a new strategy is shaped into the decisive policy of operation in Book Two (lines 344-390). It is Beelzebub who finalizes the decision:

> What if we find
> Some easier enterprise? There is a place
> (If ancient and prophetic fame in Heav'n
> Err not) another World, the happy seat
> Of some new Race call'd *Man*....
>
> here perhaps
> Some advantageous act may be achiev'd
> By sudden onset, either with Hell fire
> To waste his whole Creation, or possess
> All as our own, and drive as we were driven,
> The puny habitants, or if not drive,
> Seduce them to our Party, that thir God
> May prove thir foe, and with repenting hand
> Abolish his own works.
>
> (ii. 345-370)

The epic comment on this decision reiterates the poetic theme of the continual transformation of destruction into re-creation, of evil into good (lines 380-386), for "thir spite still serves/His glory to augment."

(i. 385-386).

God's design of re-creation through temptation and fall is finally made explicit in Book Ten:

> I suffer them to enter and possess
> A place so heav'nly, and conniving seem
> To gratify my scornful Enemies,
> That laugh, as if transported with some fit
> Of Passion, I to them had quitted all,
> At random yielded up to their misrule;
> And know not that I call'd and drew them thither
> My Hell-hounds, to lick up the draff and filth
> Which man's polluting Sin with taint hath shed
> On what was pure, till cramm'd and gorg'd, nigh burst
> With suckt and glutted offal, at one sling
> Of thy victorious Arm, well-pleasing Son,
> Both *Sin*, and *Death*, and yawning *Grave* at last
> Through *Chaos* hurl'd, obstruct the mouth of Hell
> For ever, and seal up his ravenous Jaws.
> Then Heav'n and Earth renew'd shall be made pure
> To sanctity that shall receive no stain.
>
> (x. 623-639)

Satan's renewal of the challenge against God, through the instrumentality of man, releases the two forces of love and hate which bring together the main climaxes of the narrative into a pattern of love-and-hate antithesis. These two emotions alternately pulse through the epic plot controlling the rhythms of movements, establishing the major contrasts. The "Love-Hate" opposition shapes itself as the emotional theme of the poem as the epic action proceeds.

Each of these emotions of love and hate draws towards it, as in a vortex, all associated feelings. The emotional spectra of *Paradise Lost* can be comprehended under the two broad captions of "Love" and "Hate". The "Challenge-and-Response" theme of mythology is translated in the epic into the theme of the antithesis between love and hate. Each Book of *Paradise Lost* can be characterized in terms of its dominating energy, either of love or of hate.

Books One and Two generate the energy of hate, and are controlled by it. The first description of Satan's eyes in Book One is:

> round he throws his baleful eyes

> That witness'd huge affliction and dismay
> Mixt with obdùrate pride and steadfast hate:
>
> (i. 56-58)

Later in the same book, the Love-versus-Hate motif is repeated in the lines:

> How all his malice serv'd but to bring forth
> Infinite goodness, grace and mercy shown
> On Man....
>
> (i. 217-219)

It is echoed in Book Two by Moloch, "as not behind in hate" (line 120), and re-echoed later by Beelzebub in the lines:

> and what peace can we return,
> But to our power hostility and hate,
> Untam'd reluctance, and revenge though slow,
>
> (ii. 335-337)

The antithetical emotion of love (with its correlates of Grace, Mercy, and Joy) begins to operate in Book Three which is the Book of Celestial Love, as Book Two is the Book of Hellish Hate. The emotional contrast begins to operate when God the Almighty Father from Heaven surveys Earth and Heaven and

> On Earth he first beheld
> Our two first Parents, yet the only two
> Of mankind, in the happy garden plac't
> Reaping immortal fruits of joy and love,
> Uninterrupted joy, unrivall'd love
> In blissful solitude.
>
> (iii. 64-68)

What God seeks for in Man is "true allegiance, constant Faith or Love" (line 104). Divine Love is felt in its Radiant Reflection in God the Son:

> Beyond compare the Son of God was seen
> Most glorious, in him all his Father shone

> Substantially express'd, and in his face
> Divine compassion visibly appear'd,
> Love without end, and without measure Grace.
>
> (iii. 138-142)

The characterization of God the Son, as the poetic realization of Love is continued throughout Book Three, and in Book Eleven (lines 20-45). God's problem in Book Three is:

> Say Heav'nly Powers, where shall we find such love,
> Which of ye will be mortal to redeem
> Man's mortal crime, and just th' unjust to save,
> Dwells in all Heaven charity so dear?
>
> (iii. 213-216)

The answer is that it dwells in the Son of God, "In whom the fulness dwells of love divine" (iii. 224-225), and who is the "means" for God's "Grace". God the Son breathes "immortal love/to mortal men" (iii. 267-268). Through this immortal Love, and the sacrificial death of God the Son, Man is re-created.

> So Man, as is most just,
> Shall satisfy for Man, be judg'd and die,
> And dying rise, and rising with him raise
> His Brethren, ransom'd with his own dear life.
> So Heav'nly love shall outdo Hellish hate,
>
> (iii. 294-298)

The sacrificial mediation and humiliation will vindicate the principle of Divine Being in God the Son, for in Him

> Love hath abounded more than Glory abounds,
> Therefore thy Humiliation shall exalt
> With thee thy Manhood also to this Throne;
>
> (iii. 312-314)

Set against this background of Heavenly Love is Satan the Hellish Hate, already portrayed in Books One and Two, whose "unconquerable will" contains the "study of revenge" and "immortal hate" (i. 106-107). In fact we can only conceive of the characterizations of God the Son and Satan as Heavenly Love and Hellish Hate respectively. All other attributes are subsumed under the operative conception of these two emotional principles.

From the Infernal and Celestial dimensions of the earlier Books, as we pass to the terrestrial dimension of Books Four, Five, Seven, Eight and Nine, the human interest in the theme of love develops. The Heavenly and Hellish abstractions of Love, and Hate are transformed and localized in the human context. Love produces two orientations in man, both tending towards the establishment of an ontological identity, first, of man with himself, exemplified in the relation between Adam and Eve, and second, of man as the divine image of and likeness with his Maker.

The life of bliss and joy portrayed as paradise is nothing but the condition of man's integrity with himself and the Author of his Being, a state of existence reflected in many subsidiary details such as man's wisdom, his dominion over the rest of creation, freedom from fear, anxiety, and sorrow, hope of immortality, the conjugal happiness of Adam and Eve, the rationality of man, the stateliness and the glory of his appearance, and the pleasure and dignity of labour. These details together constitute the descriptive content of the Biblical sentence: "So God created man in his own image, in the image of God created he him."

In Book Four, in Satan's soliloquy (lines 33 ff.) the recurrence of the love-versus-hate antithesis sets in bold relief the pictorial effects of Paradise as the seat of love, and Hell as the seat of Hate. The internal chaos of Satan's mind, his "mental" hell is set against "A Heaven on Earth: for blissful Paradise/Of God the Garden of Eden was" (iv. 208-209). The contrast is re-inforced in every psychological detail. Satan's remorse and self-criticism is this:

Hadst thou the same free Will and Power to stand?
Thou hadst: whom hast thou then or what to accuse,
But Heav'n's free Love dealt equally to all?
Be then his Love accurst, since love or hate,
To me alike, it deals eternal woe.

(iv. 66-70)

The interior hell he suffers is more dreadful than the physical hell.

Me miserable! which way shall I fly

Infinite wrath, and infinite despair?
Which way I fly is Hell; myself am Hell;
And in the lowest deep a lower deep
Still threat'ning to devour me opens wide.

(iv. 73-77)

The picture of this psychological hell, bottomless hate and despair, is created to emphasize, through contrast, its opposite: the Garden of Eden and God's image and likeness in it. Structurally, the technique of contrasting Satan's Hellish Hate and his physiognomy which this determines, with Paradise and its human agents, is maintained throughout Book Four, and throughout it, Satan is present as a spy in every scene, providing the foil of contrast. Passions disfigure Satan's personality and it is no longer heroic.

Thus while he spake, each passion dimm'd his face,
Thrice chang'd with pale, ire, envy and despair,
Which marr'd his borrow'd visage.

(iv. 114-116)

Immediately follows the description of Paradise and the Godlike majesty and beauty of Adam and Eve, who though "Not spirit, yet to heav'nly spirits bright/Little inferior", and whom even Satan "could love" (lines 36 ff). The dialogues between Adam and Eve in Book Four and Five are variations on the theme of Love, that is, love of God, and mutual love between Adam and Eve, interspersed with the bitterness of Satan's self-destructive hatred and his bitter regrets.

Structurally, one of the most crucial passages of the epic occurs in Book Four. Because of its importance we must quote it in full:

Sight hateful, sight tormenting! thus these two
Imparadis't in one another's arms
The happier *Eden*, shall enjoy thir fill
Of bliss on bliss, while I to Hell am thrust,
Where neither joy nor love, but fierce desire,
Among our other torments not the least,
Still unfulfill'd with pain of longing pines;
Yet let me not forget what I have gain'd
From thir own mouths; all is not theirs it seems:

> One fatal Tree there stands of Knowledge call'd,
> Forbidden them to taste: Knowledge forbidd'n?
> Suspicious, reasonless. Why should thir Lord
> Envy them that? can it be sin to know,
> Can it be death? and do they only stand
> By Ignorance, is that thir happy state,
> The proof of thir obedience and thir faith?
> O fair foundation laid whereon to build
> Thir ruin! Hence I will excite thir minds
> With more desire, to know, and to reject
> Envious commands, invented with design
> To keep them low whom Knowledge might exalt
> Equal with Gods; aspiring to be such,
> They taste and die: what likelier can ensue?
>
> (iv. 505-527)

These lines conceal the most powerful dramatic irony in the whole poem. Up to this moment Satan has not evolved the technique of his temptation; his plans for revenge are vague. Ironically, Satan hears of the interdicted Tree of Knowledge, and of the sole prohibition except for which man has unrestricted rule over Paradise, from Adam's dialogue with his wife. The tragic irony is deepened when we understand that the first reference to the Tree of Knowledge occurs in the first matrimonial conversation between Adam and Eve, "when *Adam* first of men/To first of Women Eve thus moving speech" (iv. 407-410). Ironically too, one of the two reasons which Adam sets forth to Eve why Man ought to love and obey God always is that God

>   requires
> From us no other service than to keep
> This one, this easy charge, of all the Trees
> In Paradise that bear delicious fruit
> So various, not to taste that only Tree
> Of Knowledge, planted by the Tree of Life,
> So near grows Death to Life, whate'er Death is,
> Some dreadful thing no doubt; for well thou know'st
> God hath pronounc't death to taste that Tree....
>   Then let us not think hard
> One easy prohibition we enjoy

Free leave so large, to all things else, and choice
Unlimited of manifold delights:
But let us ever praise Him, and extol
His bounty....

(iv. 419-437)

The poetic paradox is that the very fact which Adam adduces as reason for obeying and loving God is turned into the central device in the technique of temptation. Satan overhears these words of Adam. He has now chosen the particular mode of winning man to his allegiance. He has also been able to decide upon the target of his persuasive operations, Eve. From this passage, Satan learns that Eve would prove weaker when tempted. All his thoughts now tend to the task of separating Eve, physically and emotionally from Adam. So he prepares to work upon Eve's consciousness during sleep through a dream.

Assaying by his Devilish art to reach
The Organs of her Fancy, and with them forge
Illusions as he list, Phantasms and Dreams,
Or if, inspiring venom, he might taint
Th' animal spirits that from pure blood arise
Like gentle breaths from Rivers
          pure, thence raise
At least distemper'd, discontended thoughts,
Vain hopes, vain aims, inordinate desires
Blown up with high conceits ingend'ring pride.

(iv. 801-809)

To those who are determined in locating the cause of the fall in human nature, I may point out that Adam's garrulousness, his romantic talkativeness, can be adduced as the most convincing reason for the fall, on the evidence of the text. This argument may seem frivolous, but no more frivolous than the other proposed causes of the fall. For if Adam had not explained in detail to Eve the nature of the "sole prohibition", then Satan would not have come to know of the interdicted Tree and this knowledge enabled him to devise the most irresistible source of temptation. Satan has overheard that

One fatal Tree there stands of Knowledge call'd,

> Forbidden them to taste: Knowledge forbidd'n?
> Suspicious, reasonless. Why should thir Lord
> Envy them that? can it be sin to know,
> Can it be death? and do they only stand
> By Ignorance, is that thir happy state,
> The proof of thir obedience and thir faith?
> O fair foundation laid whereon to build
> Thir ruin!
>
> (iv. 514-522)

Knowledge of this "firm foundation" whereon to lay their ruin comes to Satan from Adam himself. Satan's main problem, after his defeat in the Celestial War, was to discover the forms of the new challenge which he was to offer God through the medium of His creature, and from this very creature himself, came that suggestion which Satan exploited successfully in Book Nine.

Having decided upon the overall strategy of the new attack Satan is quick to work out the successive steps in it.

> Hence I will excite thir minds
> With more desire to know, and to reject
> Envious commands, invented with design
> To keep them low whom Knowledge might exalt
> Equal with Gods; aspiring to be such,
> They taste and die: what likelier can ensue?
>
> (iv. 522-527)

This decision directly leads to Eve's dream (in lines 799-809). Milton's conception of an ideal married life centres around the fellowship of "happy conversation", and it might appear somewhat humorous that in this very "happy conversation", Adam lays the foundation, before his honeymoon in Eden is over, for the ruin of his matrimonial fellowship and happy conversation with Eve.

In this climactic context Milton seems to be illustrating that ambivalence which is intrinsic in all human situations, their inherent antithetical potentialities for good and evil. Life's moral task would be, in Milton's ethics, the suppression of the one, and the development of the other.

The first action of Adam in Eden is that of instructing Eve in the felicity of human life, and in the conditions which can eternalize this felicity. Adam's action here is not dictated by the necessity of his psychology. It arises from the structural necessity in the narrative, for in Milton's treatment of the Genesis myth, the prohibition against the Tree of Knowledge is communicated to Adam alone by God. Eve was created after the moral injunction had been given to Adam (see Book Eight, lines 321-490). I have dwelt at length on this epic incident, Adam's first dialogue with Eve in Book Four, to illustrate the progress of the narrative, its interrelated development from correlated incidents through the structural principle of antithesis and contrast till the entire action climaxes in the crisis of the fall.

Book Four, through the technique of contrasting antithetical situations of love and hate, develops the creative principle of human love. The creativity of human love is God's only means of replenishing Heaven. The epic paean in honour of wedded love in this Book is its central theme.

> Our Maker bids increase, who bids abstain
> But our Destroyer, foe to God and Man?
> Hail wedded Love, mysterious Law, true source
> Of human offspring, sole propriety
> In Paradise of all things common else.
> By thee adulterous lust was driv'n from men
> Among the bestial herds to range, by thee
> Founded in Reason, Loyal, Just and Pure,
> Relations dear, and all the Charities
> Of Father, Son, and Brother first were known.
>
> (iv. 748-757)

This "Perpetual Fountain of Domestic Sweets" in which, according to Milton, lies the essence of conjugal felicity continues to flow with some interruptions now and then till Book Nine.

Since we are now tracing the course of love in the poem we must pass over rapidly the celestial dialogue between Raphael and Adam in Books Five, Six, and Seven. Their relevance in the narrative is no longer critically disputed, and thus they need not concern us here. The first interruption in the continual flow of love is subconscious. The dream which Eve describes in the beginning of Book Five is a vague anticipation of its complete cessation at the fall in Book Nine. It anticipates the fall in several ways: first, through a vague suggestiveness, dim forebodings that the subconscious reality of the dream might be translated into actuality; second, through descriptive parallelism, for, the full epic narration of the fall in Book Nine is a heightened elaboration of the contents of Eve's dream; third, the dream itself is the prologue to the fall; while it is neither the fall, nor its cause, yet it stands in an integral relationship to that final event. On the subconscious level, it gives proof that Satan has succeeded in the first stage of temptation. Thus, it is the beginning of that process of disastrous separation between Adam and Eve. The dream of Eve seems to show a potency, not easily understood in terms of Adam's "Seventeenth-Century" Faculty psychology, according to which

> Evil into the mind of God or Man
> May come and go, so unapprov'd, and leave
> No spot or blame behind; Which gives me hope
> That what in sleep thou didst abhor to dream,
> Waking thou never wilt consent to do.
> (v. 117-121)

Adam's hope has been belied. There are more things in a dream than are thought of in Seventeenth-Century psychology. But before we dwell at length on the connection between the dream in Book Four and its narration in Book Five, and the actual fall itself, we must conclude our discussion of the theme of love, by referring to its treatment in Book Eight. In this Book of the epic as in Book Four the theme is human love, its true nature, and the forms of its manifestation in thought, feeling, and action; and the reciprocity of the moral obligations it imposes upon man.

Adam's description of his own creation, in terms of the contents of his memory immediately after his creation (in Book Eight, lines 253 to 357) as God's image and likeness, leads to the meaning of that very concept. Man has been created in God's image and similitude. As such he embodies the principle of happiness and, as we have seen earlier, the capacity to experience blissful happiness is part of the element of man's nature as divine likeness. So the "humanness" of Adam is not complete till his happiness is complete. A fellow human being, sexually differentiated to ensure the union of the body with the communion of the spirit, is necessary to complete that conception of man as God's image. So Adam asks,

> In solitude
> What happiness, who can enjoy alone,
> Or all enjoying, what contentment find?
>
> (viii. 364-366)

Adam asks for a partner in life, not for the sake of the pleasure of the sense "whereby mankind/Is propagated," but because of his awareness that his own being and nature are not completed except in the immediacy of personal relationship. The intensity of equal society, and the participation through fellowship in all rational delights are pre-conditions for man's happiness. Denied these, man does not attain to the status of God's image. The need for another being to complete and complement human nature is a requirement of man's very being, so that apart from this, man's nature cannot be understood. The solitary individual, by himself, is deficient, and in so far as he is deficient he does not represent God's image and likeness, and human nature is not realized in the actuality of man.

In God "is no deficience found" (viii. 416), and in so far as there is a deficience in man, man is not God's image. This deficience is remedied in the fact of human relationship, in the fact that the "deficient" solitary individual can remedy his deficiency, can "complete" himself, through relating himself to another person. Thus, essentially, the human element in man is not his individuality, but this relation. And man is to be defined in terms of this relationship with other human beings. God's image and likeness in man is their relationship. Adam's expostulation with his Maker renders this meaning explicitly clear in Book Eight:

> Supreme of things;
> Thou in thyself art perfet' and in thee
> Is no deficience found; not so is Man,
> But in degree, the cause of his desire
> By conversation with his like to help,
> Or solace his defects....
> But Man by number is to manifest
> His single imperfection, and beget
> Like of his like, his Image multipli'd,

> In unity defective, which requires
> Collateral love, and dearest amity.
>
> (viii. 416-426)

God approves of this and is pleased at Adam's

> Expressing well the spirit within thee free,
> My image, not imparted to the Brute....
>   I, ere thou spak'st,
> Knew it not good for Man to be alone.
>
> (viii. 441-445)

 To our main enquiry as to the nature of man, according to Milton, the answer is to be found in his poetic extensions of the Biblical theory: "So God created man in his own image, in the image of God created he him, male and female created he them." Man's nature is defined in terms of his capacity to establish a collateral love and fellowship with other human beings. This very relationship is the nature of man, and it is the image of God. The Divine element in man's nature is in "Love", and the relation of amity towards other fellow mortals. Love completes man's being as God's image and likeness. So Adam's relationship in collateral love with Eve is his nature. In *Paradise Lost* there is no conception of human nature apart from this relationship. The poetic conception of Adam is only completed in the complementary conception of Eve. There is no Adam without Eve; no Eve without Adam. They, in their union, constitute human nature in the epic.

 Adam refers to Eve in Book Five as the "Best Image of myself and dearer half" (v. 95). Similar complimentary phrases occur throughout the poem. As I have said earlier, they are not part of the romantic vocabulary of erotic love, on the contrary they establish the theological perspectives of the poem, its theo-centric conception of man. In Book Eight, God uses the same phrase to characterize Eve.

> What next I bring shall please thee, be assur'd,
> Thy likeness, thy fit help, thy other self,
> Thy wish, exactly to thy heart's desire.
>
> (viii. 449-451)

God is not here exercising Himself in romantic hyperbole. Adam re-states this principle of oneness with Eve on seeing her.

> I now see
> Bone of my Bone, Flesh of my Flesh, my Self
> Before me: Woman is her Name, of Man
> Extracted; for this cause he shall forgo
> Father and Mother, and to his Wife adhere;
> And they shall be one Flesh, one Heart, one Soul.
> (viii. 494-499)

Having elaborated the theme of Love in terms of human nature and also having illustrated the nature of the one in terms of the other, Milton devotes the final lines of Book Eight to point the true directions in which both love and human nature should develop. Any slight suspicion of a tendency on Adam's part to equate love with pleasure is rebuked by the Celestial Teacher:

> Love refines
> The thoughts, and heart enlarges, hath his seat
> In Reason, and is judicious, is the scale
> By which to heav'nly Love thou may'st ascend,
> Not sunk in carnal pleasure, for which cause
> Among the Beasts no Mate for thee was found.
> (viii. 589-594)

On Adam's assenting that this is the love he feels for Eve, and with Raphael's revelation that from the universal divine power of love even the angels are not exempt, the epic scene moves to the tragedy of the fall in Book Nine.

CHAPTER TWELFTH

CRISIS AND RESOLUTION IN "PARADISE LOST" MAN AS FREE AND AS FALLEN

ONE OF KIERKEGAARD's famous philosophical comments deals with the irreconcilability of man's freedom with any theoretical reconstruction of human nature. Says He: "The fact that God could create free beings *vis-a-vis* of Himself is the Cross which philosophy could not carry, but remained hanging therefrom."[1] Likewise the paradox that a free being could sin and fall through his very freedom itself is a cross from which Milton criticism is seen hanging, it being unable to support this paradox. The poetry of *Paradise Lost* achieves the impossible task of combining the concept of man's freedom with the Biblical fact of the fall of man. But when this achievement is sought to be translated into the discursive language of criticism and interpretation, criticism meets with its fate.

Criticism's main difficulty is in its failure to discover an ethical equivalent for the Fall story; but this very effort to invest an action with an ethical meaning which does not come under the scope of ethics is itself a misdirection. Sin is not a moral concept except in the very general sense of the terms. It more properly belongs in theology and psychology (defined as the study of the subjective self), in dogmatics, and in mythology. In Chapter Eight, we have seen the conflicting conclusions which all moralistic interpretations of the fall ultimately lead to.

Let us now look at the same problem, the paradox of man's fall and his essential freedom from all the relevant perspectives afresh. In the concept of the fall, there are multiple foci: there is a dimension of theology in the sense that the fall affects the God-man relationship; there is psychology in the sense that the fall is determinative for human nature after it; there is the mythological content; and in Milton's treatment of the fall in Book Nine, there is a dimension of poetic creation, a new dimension of meaning created by the poet. Criticism must therefore not seek a monistic explanation. It must on the contrary attempt a complex interpretation touching on all the layers of meaning.

[1] Quoted by M.C. Darcy, S.J. in *The Mind and Heart of Love*, p. 156.

Within the general mythical framework of the second encounter between Yahweh and the Serpent through the medium and agency of man, Milton combines the creation story of Genesis 1 with the Fall story of Genesis 3. The first encounter leads to the creation of man, the second, to his re-creation. The continuance of Satan's challenge of God gives Him (God) a continuous opportunity for re-creating human nature. When man has been fully re-created and "ingrafted" in Christ, the challenge has finally disappeared and the Dragon has been destroyed. The cycle of Withdrawal and Return is complete. The dualism of Love and Hate has collapsed in the Unity of Love. Reworking this myth in Book Nine, Milton has created a complex network of poetic intuitions and philosophical insights into human nature.

Briefly, in Milton's creative modification of the fall in the epic, the fall is a free act. Using (or misusing freedom), man leaps into action. This leap itself is the fall, and is caused by no other fact, but by the assertion of the very fact of his freedom. As a free act, as a leap into the unknown, it is no less heroic and adventurous. Poetically, the leap into the unknown is illustrated in terms of its effects.

The particular act of transgression, the eating of the fruit of the Tree of Knowledge is not itself the whole act of transgression but only its culmination and climax. Further, the transgression of man in the poem cannot be separated into two constituent units, namely, the separate transgression of Eve and Adam. The poetic conception of "man" in the poem comprehends both Adam and Eve in such a manner that what either of them does is done by man. So when Eve is fallen, Adam is also essentially fallen, and Adam's transgression is not an act of self-sacrifice and love, but the expression through repetition of the inevitable human condition already created by Eve. Further, the representation of the fall in the poem is theological, and not simply ethical. I mean that the transgression is not rendered as an evil act, and therefore as man's disobedience of God, but that it is primarily an act of disobedience and therefore evil. The theological element of disobedience is primary, and it is what makes it evil, and not the element of evil which transforms it into a creaturely rebellion against the Creator. Thus the fall, theologically conceived, implies alienation, the distancing of the relation of man from himself, and from God. In the fall what we are witnessing is the breaking down of a unity, the forcing of a rupture in an integral whole of reality, comprising God, man, and created beings.

Finally, the fall portrays the genesis of "dread" qualified as sin, in man in whom before its occurrence, innocence prevailed. Innocence is ignorance only in respect of passions. Man as God's image has wisdom and innocence at the same time, paradoxically speaking. What he did not experience was anxiety, the matrix of all passions. Through the fall what man lost is innocence—ignorance of passions. In the Kierkegaardian sense, man's leap into this very condition of "dread" is the fall, the original sin of Adam and of mankind. The fall is Original Sin in that it is "original" to all other sins, and also in that all other sins originate in it.

The fall is specifically a human act. Man falls by the very fact that he is man, and not an animal. Paradoxically, the distinctive humanity of man is proved by his ability to "fall" which the animal is not capable of. In Milton's epic, the fall is not a simple act of levity, nor is it caused by such an act. The fall is not identical with the loss of reason, nor is it precipitated through the eclipse of reason. The fall is also not identical with man's surrender to sensuality, nor does it happen through such a surrender. Man does not fall through love in any form, or its excess, though the fall implies the loss of love. The fall cannot also be equated with the usurpation of human judgment by the passions, nor does such an usurpation explain the motivation of the fall. Conceived by mythology as a free act of man, defined by theology as Original Sin, explained through psychology as the beginning of the knowledge of passions, of dread, and of anxiety, the fall can only be poetically represented in all of these aspects.

The fall of man as a free act is retrospectively viewed by God the Father in Book Ten.

> No Decree of mine
> Concurring to necessitate his Fall,
> Or touch with lightest moment of impulse
> His free Will, to her own inclining left
> In even scale.
>
> (x. 45-47)

Structurally, the fall is illustrated through the stages of alienation between Adam and Eve, first, and then between man and God.

The first stage in this separation is in the beginning of Book Eight (in lines 40-57) when Eve, seeing her husband entering on abstruse thought, voluntarily leaves the presence of Raphael and Adam. Whatever her reasons, or the reasons which the epic comment provides, her departure indicates the beginning of the end. Here is the beginning of those "high disputes" which "conjugal caresses will not solve." Indeed all conjugal caresses come to an end here. Throughout the rest of this Book she is absent from the epic scene.

With the commencement of Book Nine, the poet changes

Those Notes to Tragic; foul distrust, and breach
Disloyal on the part of Man, revolt,
And disobedience.

(x. 6-9)

And Eve has assumed not a conjugal tone, but a highly argumentative pose. After her physical separation from Adam's presence in Book Eight, we see her next emotionally alienated from Adam. That love interferes with work is the theme of her new dispute. The dispute between them now is on the primacy of love over work. For Eve, work is more fundamental than love. Being so near, looks and smiles intervene, or casual discourse on new objects intermits the day's work. So "let us divide our labours", and when Eve proposes this division, she is essentially divided with herself, and from Adam.

Adam's appeal to "love" does not go home to Eve, for the moment she has suggested the "division of labour" she has already moved in the direction of transgression. To Adam, love is the prime end of life, and not labour. God has not condemned man to hard labour. "For not to irksome toil, but to delight/He made us, and delight to Reason join'd" (ix. 242-243). The measure of the emotional alienation between Adam and Eve can be easily assessed on the basis that what Adam calls the "food of the mind", "the food of love", "this sweet intercourse/Of looks and smiles" is to Eve interference, obstruction to the task laid before them, and work is to Eve that "task", while for Adam love is not the lowest end of life.

Adam seems to be on the defensive in respect of love when he qualifies it negatively as "Love not the lowest end of life" (ix. 241), instead of positing it as one of the two highest ends of life, the other being their fealty to God. Adam's awareness that separation and severance mean danger and fall does not help him in countering Eve's decision, and this re-inforces the sense of alienation in the theory of the fall.

> But other doubt possesses me, lest harm
> Befall thee sever'd from me.
>
> (ix. 251-252)

And therefore Adam urges Eve,

> leave not the faithful side
> That gave thee being, still shades thee and protects.
>
> (ix. 265-266)

The rest of the interlocution till the fateful moment when Adam permits Eve to separate from him is a disquisition on the themes of love, reason, and virtue in the familiar terms of Seventeenth-Century Faculty psychology. Eve is finally permitted to leave Adam's presence, not without some moralising exhortations.

> Go; for thy stay, not free, absents thee more;
> Go in thy native innocence, rely
> On what thou hast of virtue, summon all.
>
> (ix. 372-374)

The poetic situation here is built up of several paradoxes. Adam knows that separation between the husband and wife at this moment is against their law of being, and that it portends the very greatest of dangers, the possibility of their defection from God, and the loss of their happiness, but he acts against his own better knowledge and conviction. This is an anticipation of his similar conduct later in the poem (x. 989-1016) when he repeats the transgression. Why does he do this? This decision is in fact, the first deliberate and conscious step taken by him in the poem. Up to this moment, Adam is described as a passive agent pouring forth the contents of his soul in songs of joy and praise to the Creator. The first existential problem is presented to him by Eve at this moment, and this, in fact, is the first time when Eve too is shown as taking a decisive step towards poetic action. Eve's is a step in the direction of separation, the departing point from a state of unity. When Eve has taken this decision, it is not only Eve but man on the whole, who is on the verge of the fall.

Eve's fall affects Adam neither magically through telepathy, nor through any mystic action at a distance. The instantaneous and simultaneous fall of Adam, at the very moment when Eve falls, is a corollary, to the poetic conception of man in *Paradise Lost*. This conception, having its origin in Genesis 1, does not treat Adam and Eve as separate individuals, and humanity is not identified with individuality—but with the relationship of community which the two individuals can and should establish. Adam by himself does not comprehend the definition of "man"; neither does Eve by herself. It is the "Adam-Eve" relationship that is comprehended in that definition of man as God's image. Man was made in God's image, and male, and female, created He them.

All theories of man can only be built on two axioms, the axiomatic assumption of human iodividuality and human community, and all variations in these theories develop in accordance with the emphasis placed on either of the assumptions. Neither could be stressed to the exclusion of the other. Epic poetry, as also religious thought—for both share the same serious concern with human history and human destiny—must reckon with the tensions between the individuality of man, and the community of human relationship which guarantees individuality, and resolve those tensions into an equilibrium of relationships. This is done, in poetry and religion, by conceiving of human reality itself as a relationship.

When man was created male and female, the sexual differentiation was not the distinctively human factor, for even animals had it, but that this very differentiation emphasized the element of relationship between two individualities. For Adam, Eve is not only the "female sex", she is the "other person". Likewise for Eve, Adam's importance is not in his sexual differentiation as a male, but in his being a partner in a human relationship. In the words of Karl Barth: "The female is to the male, and the male to the female, the other man and as such the fellow-man".[2]

In the Biblical conception of man, as also in Milton s use of it in *Paradise Lost*, humanity is always "fellow-humanity". In *Paradise Lost*, every offence against man is at the same time an offence against

[2] *Church Dogmatics*, Vol. II, pt. 4, p. 118.

God; likewise every offence against God is at the same time an offence against man. Such is the framework of its plot, that the alienation of either of the members of the human community (of Adam and Eve) is an alienation of man himself from God. When the first act of separation has been completed, Eve is no longer the "matrimonial accomplish't Eve", "the best image of Adam", and the "dearer half". There is neither grace in all her steps, nor "Heav'n in her Eye". The image and similitude of God in her has already begun to be eclipsed. The bitterness of her resentment (ix. 273-289) at Adam's concern for her safety, and her argumentativeness have begun to present a character of Eve, fully realized later in the Temptation episode.

> But that thou shouldst my firmness therefore doubt
> To God or thee, because we have a foe
> May tempt it, I expected not to hear.
>   (ix. 279-281)

Her unrelenting insistence on the implied affront to her dignity likewise augurs her mental disposition at the time of the fall, and the arguments by which she acquiesces in Satan's temptation:

> His fraud is then thy fear, which plain infers
> Thy equal fear that my firm Faith and Love
> Can by his fraud be shak'n or seduc't;
> Thoughts, which how found they harbor in thy breast,
> *Adam*, misthought of her to thee so dear?
>   (ix. 285-289)

It is true that if Eve had not been granted permission to go, the final fall would not have occurred. Then, was Adam right in granting her freedom to separate herself from him? On one level of meaning, Adam was wrong in granting this freedom, and in acting against his own knowledge, he was not acting firmly or ethically in the sense that he was abdicating his responsibility as the head of the family. Thus in one sense Adam has done a wrong by this very act, and in so far as he has done a wrong, he has begun to lapse from his true nature as God's image. Similarly, Eve, by asking for freedom, whatever the reason or pretext, was wrong, and she has compromised her divine similitude. This epic scene, thus, of the first conjugal dispute (lines 205-404) is not only a dramatic anticipation of the fall, but is itself the first rupture of relations between man and woman, a disunity raised to the metaphysical proportions of man's creaturely rebellion against God, and therefore the first step in the fall. This is the beginning of that foul distrust, and "breach disloyal on the part of man", revolt, and disobedience, and

> On the part of Heav'n
> Now alienated, distance and distaste,
> Anger and just rebuke, and judgment giv'n,
> That brought into this World a world of woe,
> Sin and her shadow Death, and Misery
> Death's Harbinger.
>
> (ix. 8-13)

"Love thy neighbour as thyself" is a theological imperative as important as the first commandment, "Love thy Lord God with all thy heart". Adam and Eve (as the only two representatives of humanity in the Epic) sum up all human relationships: the neighbourly, in so far as to Adam, Eve is the "other person", and to Eve, Adam is the other person; and the conjugal relationship of husband and wife. A crisis in their love is man's first transgression of the divine command to love one's neighbour as one self, and also the command that man and wife shall be "one Flesh, one Heart, one Soul" (viii. 499), and that man should not put asunder what God has joined. Having transgressed two divine commands in the one act of transgressive separation, the transgression in respect of the Tree of Knowledge is only the completion of the fall.

Two long passages intervene between Eve's hapless departure from Adam's presence, and the fatal event at noon. The epic voice (lines 404-443), through its comments on the tragic irony implicit in the situation, connects this incident with the fall. Satan's spiteful soliloquy (in lines 444-493) establishes the "love-hate" antithesis in the poem. Eve's beauty, her "Heav'nly form/Angelic", and "Her graceful Innocence, her every Air/ Of gesture or least action overaw'd/His Malice". For a short space, beauty overcomes the evil in Satan, and he remains stunned, "stupidly good".

> That space the Evil one abstracted stood
> From his own evil, and for the time remain'd

> Stupidly good, of enmity disarm'd,
> Of guile, of hate, of envy, of revenge.
>
> (ix. 463-466)

Love for a moment is supreme even in Satan's mind, but hate soon re-asserts itself. "But the hot Hell that always in him burns.../ Soon ended his delight," and Satan remembers that "What brought us [here is] hate, not love."

This is one of the most dramatic parts of the whole epic. The continuous conflict between love and hate has nowhere else been brought into so sharp a focus as Love's overawing influence on hate for a short while, and hate's resilience in immediately re-asserting itself are both concentrated in the immediate moment of confrontation (ix. 463-493).

> Shee fair, divinely fair, fit Love for Gods,
> Not terrible, though terror be in Love
> And beauty, not approacht by stronger hate,
> Hate stronger, under show of Love well feign'd.
>
> (ix. 489-492)

Here we come upon the problem of all problems in Milton Criticism which has already been referred to. Critics have always been puzzled by a certain degree of unanalysable complexity in Milton's treatment of the fall episode in *Paradise Lost* which is its epic crisis. In the treatment of the fall theme there seems to subsist an ambiguity. The poetry and the ethics of the theme do not appear to cohere. The inevitable logic of the narrative develops in a direction, contrary to the direction the moral judgments on the situation point. The fall is morally condemned by the poet. It is everywhere in the poem "foul distrust, and breech disloyal on the part of Man", and "revolt, and disobedience." It brought into the "World a world of woe,/Sin and her shadow Death, and Misery/Death's Harbinger...." The transgressive act of Eve herself is lamented by the poet after Eve's fall:

> So saying, her rash hand in evil hour
> Forth reaching to the Fruit, she pluck'd, she eat:
> Earth felt the wound and Nature from her seat
> Sighing through all her Works gave signs of woe,

That all was lost.

> (ix. 780-784)

Original sin is completed with Adam's transgression. Earth trembled from her entrails, as again, in pangs, and Nature gave a second groan.

> Sky low'r'd, and muttering Thunder, some sad drops
> Wept at completing of the mortal Sin
> Original.
>
> (ix. 1002-1004)

But when we scrutinize the motives of both transgressions, we find nothing condemnatory. Eve is prompted by the "not-wholly-undesirable" motive of rebellion against an arbitrary and unseasonable imposition (iv. 745-794). In her decision to involve Adam too in her act, along with a pardonable degree of selfishness, and transcending this selfishness at the same time, is her love for Adam.

> Confirm'd then I resolve,
> *Adam* shall share with me in bliss or woe:
> So dear I love him, that with him all deaths
> I could endure, without him live no life.
>
> (ix. 830-833)

She persuades Adam through the vehemence of her love to taste of the fruit of the forbidden Tree. No thought or action of Eve can be condemned, from the human point of view, unless we assume the unfeeling rigour of Puritan fundamentalism.

As with Eve, so with Adam, in a greater degree. His decision to concur with Eve's action, no matter what the consequences, is heroism of the highest order and it issues from the noblest of human sentiments, self-sacrificing love, love in the highest sense as we know. Adam says:

> For with thee
> Certain my resolution is to Die:
> How can I live without thee, how forgo
> Thy sweet Converse and Love so dearly join'd....
>
> (ix. 906-909)

This is the noblest situation which life or poetry can offer. The unifying power of love is tested against the power of Death.

> no no, I feel
> The Link of Nature draw me: Flesh of Flesh,
> Bone of my Bone thou art, and from thy State
> Mine never shall be parted, bliss or woe.
>
> (ix. 913-916)

Even after slow deliberation of what transgression means, Adam re-affirms his resolve:

> So forcible within my heart I feel
> The Bond of Nature draw me to my own,
> My own in thee, for what thou art is mine;
> Our State cannot be sever'd, we are one,
> One Flesh; to lose thee were to lose myself.
>
> (ix. 955-959)

Eve, even in her fallen condition, can nobly respond to the nobility of Adam's love:

> O glorious trial of exceeding Love,
> Illustrious evidence, example high....
> One Heart, one Soul in both; whereof good proof
> This day affords.
>
> (ix. 961 ff.)

No one can deny that Milton's poetry presents the fall of man in a perspective not consistent with the moral judgments on the contexts. The passages above present the highest reaches of the narrative movements in the poem. But Milton, the moralist, as the critics argue, intrudes and pronounces judgments which the reader cannot concur with. The epic comment on Adam's act of love is as follows:

> he scrupl'd not to eat
> Against his better knowledge, not deceiv'd,
> But fondly overcome with Female charm.
>
> (ix. 997-999)

This, they say, is a forced judgement which the poetry of the situation does not elicit, as irrelevant in the denunciation of the transgressive fall as sin, which in terms of our known moral ideas, it is not.

All departures in Milton criticism originate at this point in the presentation of the fall. The very ambiguity of Milton's treatment of the theme defies the formulation of an exclusive monistic theory of the fall, and of human nature. It was this purpose which led Edwin Greenlaw in "A Better Teacher than Aquinas" to argue "that *Paradise Lost* not less than the *Faerie Queene* is a moral allegory, not merely poetical theology."[3] According to him the entire presentation of the fall proves that Milton's

> Philosophy is from Greece, not from Genesis, for this choice (of good over evil) involves abstaining through temperance, the rational principle of the soul, or yielding through excess, the irrational principle. Adam fell because the irrational principle in his soul, inflamed by a provoking object, triumphed over temperance not because he disobeyed "a whimsical Tyrant", all of whose laws are arbitrary and occasional...."[4]

Having said this, Greenlaw was convinced that he defended Milton (against Raleigh). The truth is that this kind of inept defence is paradoxically the worst denunciation of Milton. It postulates Milton's poetical concerns as morality and nothing but morality. Whether on the basis of Plato or of Ethics, to treat the fall as a study in the ethical disciplining of man is at once untrue (to the evidences which the poem supplies), and uncritical. To treat the fall from a purely ethical standpoint is a critical perversity persisting even in our time. As against this tendency, Waldock's theory that the relevant emotions at the time of the fall are the noblest is a genuine critical discovery. But where we disagree with Waldock is in his conclusion that in the elaboration of the fall, the poetry develops independently of the theme.

We cannot concede that there is an irreconcilability between the epic comments on the poetic situations, and the situations themselves, an incompatibility between epic achievement and epic intention, and between myth and theme, and that "*Paradise Lost* cannot

---

[3] *Studies in Philology*, xiv (April, 1917), p. 199.
[4] *Ibid.*, pp. 200-1.

take the strain at its centre, it breaks there, the theme is too much for it."[5] On the contrary in the crisis of *Paradise Lost* inheres a complexity which demands multiple points of view and multiple approaches. Several layers of meanings telescope into the unity of its theme. It is proof of Milton's incomparable poetic power to have selected an appropriate myth for this epic which can take the strain of multiple meanings, and work them into its texture.

The crisis of the fall elicits multivocal response, a response on the level of the myth, another on the theological level, and yet another on the psychological level, and finally on the level of a simple common sense reaction. When we bear in mind the mythic framework in which the fall of man (comprising the separate falls of Eve and Adam) is located, this very framework generates a moral ambiguity at the moment of the fall. At the exact moment of the fall, the Devil wins the challenge, and it is the only moment when man is wholly in co-operation with the Devil. But this very moment of co-operation between man and the Devil is also the very same opportunity at which God can begin the task of recreating man without interfering with his freedom. It is also the beginning of history, the transition from a static condition to a dynamic process of development through complication. So the fall of man is a paradox; it is not the complete victory of Satan, but only the moment of his seeming victory and this very moment marks the beginning of his final overthrow.

In the epic, the treatment of the fall incorporates both negative and positive responses. To say this is not to bring in the theory of the fortunate fall, in a different terminology. It elucidates the elements of the myth implicit in it. In terms of the "Love and Hate" antithesis in the poem the fall as the culmination of hate is only momentary. Love re-asserts itself in some form or other. Satan's technique of temptation is to introduce and transplant the principle of hate in the human heart. Love and beauty can be "terrible" even for the Devil. So the Devil plans to match love and beauty with stronger hate. Seeing Eve, Satan sharpens his power of hate:

Shee fair, divinely fair, fit Love for Gods,
Not terrible, though terror be in Love
And beauty, not approacht by stronger hate,

[5] A.J.A. Waldock, *op. cit.*, p. 56.

Hate stronger, under show of Love well feign'd,
The way which to her ruin now I tend.

(ix. 489-493)

Though there is terror in love and beauty, Satan pretends not to be terrified for the terror of love is opposed by the greater terror of his hate. But in spite of arming himself with the terror of hate, the power of love and beauty overwhelms. In one of the most dramatic of all the descriptions in the epic, Milton presents Satan for a moment deprived of his hate, guile, malice and revenge under the overpowering impact of beauty.

> her Heav'nly form
> Angelic, but more soft, and feminine,
> Her graceful Innocence, her every Air
> Of gesture or least action overaw'd
> His Malice, and with rapine sweet bereav'd
> His fierceness of the fierce intent it brought:
> That space the Evil one abstracted stood
> From his own evil, and for the time remain'd
> Stupidly good, of enmity disarm'd,
> Of guile, of hate, of envy, of revenge;

(iv. 457-466)

The thematic significance, as also the poetic power, of this passage has been overlooked by almost all, if not all the critics. It dramatically sums up and presents the theme in a few lines, the ultimate victory of love and beauty over hate and evil. This is the only passage in which Satan is shown as "bereav'd" of his evil, but of goodness he is incapable; at most, he can be "stupidly" good. However strong Satan's "hate" may have been it is overthrown immediately in its encounter with God's image of love and beauty, i.e. Eve, who is the "Fairest resemblance of the Maker fair" (ix. 538). These lines anticipate the outcome of the "Love-hate" encounter.

At the supreme moment of hate's triumph, the moment of the fall of Eve and Adam, love still asserts itself, though not in its purest or best form. Even though tainted with selfishness and jealousy, even at the moment of the fall, the principle of love asserts itself. A.J.A. Waldock is most emphatically right when he detects the presence of love, our noblest emotion, even at the crisis of the transgression of Eve; but he is most emphatically wrong when a causal role is attributed to the emotions of love as if "love" caused the fall. The quality of love is present in Eve and Adam at the moment of the fall. But they *do not* fall because of this quality of love. The presence of love only shows that the power of hate has not been able to utterly efface this element of godlikeness in man even at the moment of its utmost triumph. Although the fall implied, through rebellion, the loss of the power of love in its best manifestations, it is still present in Adam and Eve through the very fact that they are still human. The fall does not (because it cannot) destroy the human status, God's image and likeness in man; it is only disfigured and reduced.

Paradoxically, therefore, the sentiment of love which Eve and Adam exhibit at the fall, and before and after it, is the poetic assertion of the supremacy of the principle of love, even at moments when hate seems supreme. Thus the fall illustrates the basic theme of *Paradise Lost*, the theme of love. No other myth could so well have comprehended this complex theme, and clothed it with the truth of fiction.

True, the love expressed by man at the fall is selfish, not unambiguous; is it "creaturely" and directed toward created beings. But, it is the human analogue of the Divine love for fallen man. One of the basic theological data of the epic is that God so loved the sinner that for his sake He became man and suffered and died and this principle cannot be overlooked when assessing the structural relevance of any expression of love in *Paradise Lost*. When Adam resolves to die with Eve,

> he his Love
> Had so ennobl'd, as of choice to incur
> Divine displeasure for her sake, or Death.
>
> (iii. 991-993)

Adam is only dimly and distantly reflecting, on the human plane, in the context of sin, and under the limitations imposed by his own sin, what God the Son in Book Three demonstrates:

> Behold mee then, mee for him, life for life
> I offer, on mee let thine anger fall;

Account mee man; I for his sake will leave
Thy bosom, and this glory next to thee
Freely put off, and for him lastly die.

(iii. 236-240)

This is again repeated in Book Eleven, after the fall,

       my Merit those
Shall perfet, and for these my Death shall pay.

(xi. 35-36)

It is not blasphemy to institute this analogy between the absolute perfection of Divine Love, and the sinful imperfection of human love. The differences between the two are absolute, as the agents of love are absolutely different in that that the One is the Creator and the other the creature. But as God the Son is the Head of mankind, and of the Church, so is Adam on the human plane the head of the family. So Adam's love for Eve, though tainted with sin, and expressing itself in and through sin, is nevertheless an analogue of the Divine Love. The love which Adam expresses before the fall and at the moment of the fall is not the cause of the fall, but the very principle which sustains his humanity, God's image and likeness in man even at the moment of his transgression.

But for this love, humanity would have been utterly lost at the fall; man would have destroyed himself by his total alienation from the Divine Similitude. On account of this love, man has merited the love of redemption. In fact, this very quality of love anticipates the power of repentance at the end of Book Ten.

     they forthwith to the place
Repairing where he judg'd them prostrate fell
Before him reverent, and both confess'd
Humbly thir faults, and pardon begg'd, with tears
Watering the ground, and with thir sighs the Air
Frequenting, sent from hearts contrite, in sign
Of sorrow unfeign'd, and humiliation meek.

(x. 1098-1105)

Book Ten purifies this love of its elements of selfishness and jealousy, when Adam forgives Eve. This is the resolution of the crisis in

Paradise Lost.

> But rise, let us no more contend, nor blame
> Each other, blam'd enough elsewhere, but strive
> In offices of Love, how we may light'n
> Each other's burden in our share of woe;
>
> (x. 958-961)

Eve is reconciled to Adam:

> Restor'd by thee, vile as I am, to place
> Of new acceptance, hopeful to regain
> Thy Love, the sole contentment of my heart
> Living or dying....
>
> (x. 971-975)

For Adam and Eve, mutual reconciliation is complete here. The long breach in the conjugal union of Adam and Eve, begun in Book Nine and heightened through their separation, is obliterated. The "atonement" of Man, the restoration of Eve by Adam, is the precondition for man's restoration by God, and his atonement.

This, then, is the theme of *Paradise Lost.* It is the theme of Love, in every form of its manifestation from the lowest to the highest human expression of it, and to the absolute perfection of its Divine Similitude in God the Son.

There remain two minor problems; the nature of the epic comments on Adam's fall, and the separate falls of Eve and Adam. The two epic comments in Book Nine appear to express Milton's moral judgments on Adam's action in concurring through love with Eve in the act of transgression.

> he scrupl'd not to eat
> Against his better knowledge, not deceiv'd
> But fondly overcome with Female charm.
>
> (ix. 997-999)

This, and the concluding observation, "Thus it shall befall/Him who to worth in Woman overtrusting/Lets her Will rule...." (ix. 1182-1184) do not express Milton's own moral judgements. It is quite clear from the content that it is not the poet's interpretation of the moral of the Fall. These are, in their contents, etiological responses which any reader, will make on the primeval act, from the vantage point of history. They are not the poet's moral judgements, but the historical retrospection on the first misfortune of mankind. The epic poet is here speaking for and on behalf of humanity. It is a comment on one level of meaning.

Coming to the second problem of the separate acts of transgression by Eve and Adam, we should note that the former is not the cause of the latter. They are only two aspects, or the two stages of the same act of transgression. The mythological theme of *Paradise Lost* is neither the fall of Adam, nor of Eve, but the fall of man. The epic concept of man embraces both in such a manner that the fall of either is the same as the fall of the other. When Eve is fallen, without any intervening psychological impulsion, Adam is also affected by her condition and is determined as fallen. The long process of reflection by Adam (ix. 920-989) only elucidates and illustrates the fallen condition of his interior, a condition to be exteriorized in the physical act of the eating of the forbidden fruit. "That the link of Nature draw me...." (ix. 914), and that "The Bond of Nature draw me to my own" (ix. 956) are expressions of the metaphysics of the situation. Adam's soliloquy only illustrates for the reader his interior.

There is yet another perspective and dimension of meaning in which the fall can be viewed and interpreted in the narrative context, that is, the intellectual-psychological implications of the fall. The transgression is a deliberate human act in search of knowledge and wisdom. On the level of the subjective consciousness of Adam and Eve, how is the fall to be interpreted ? As man's point of departure from innocence and ignorance, the treatment of the fall in the poem elicits multivocal response. It elicits simultaneously the antithetical responses of attraction and repulsion. As man's adventure into the realm of knowledge and wisdom, it commands admiration. At the same time, as a leap into the unknown, it begets dread. The poetic treatment of the fall evokes sympathetic antipathy, and antipathetic sympathy, at once. From the poem, it is impossible to deduce univocally Milton's attitude to knowledge.

The basic ambivalence inherent in man's quest for knowledge is captured by Milton's poetic representation. Man's quest for experience, and the more and more knowledge of it he gains, the greater his nostalgia for the lost condition of blissful innocence. The Tree of Knowledge of Good and Evil is not only forbidden, but is equally forbidding. At the same time it draws man with an irresistible pull. On the plane of man's consciousness the fall operates as the experience of dread. Before the fall, human consciousness is in a state of bliss and unconscious identity with God and the environment. Man as God's image and likeness is wise before the fall, but is equally innocent, innocent of the passions, and innocence is a form of ignorance, ignorance of evil. The fall is the moment, psychologically speaking, when man feels the dread of passions. Book Ten presents Adam and Eve as seeking after knowledge of the passions.

> Love was not in thir looks, either to God
> Or to each other, but apparent guilt,
> And shame, and perturbation, and despair,
> Anger, and obstinacy, and hate, and guile.
>
> (x. 111-114)

Milton's exploitation of the psychological implications of the fall story has modern parallels. The closest parallelism is in Soren Kierkegaard's treat of the fall and Original Sin in the *Concept of Dread*. Kierkegaard's analysis of the fall (of man) can be fruitfully used to elucidate some paradoxes of Milton's interpretation of the fall in the epic. Kierkegaards's *Concept of Dread* is a dialectical interpretation on the subject of the fall of man characterized in theology as Original Sin. Briefly, his theory emphasizes the elements of human freedom in the act of transgression. The fall is a free act of transition from a state of simplicity and innocence to a state of complication and development. It is Original Sin in the sense that it is anterior to all other experiences. It is essentially the first consciousness in the human mind of dread. Dread of what? Of freedom which is man's constitutive principle. The experience of dread immediately posits that of guilt.

In one place especially, Kierkegaard's interpretation comes very close to that of Milton. Dealing with the concept of the fall, Kierkegaard says that "the command itself prohibiting Adam to eat of the tree of knowledge engendered sin in him."[6] The prohibition, he continues, predisposes what breaks out in Adam's qualitative

[6] *Op. cit.*, p. 36.

leap.⁷ Milton' Eve praises the Tree of Knowledge as follows:

> Thy praise hee also who forbids thy use,
> Conceals not from us, naming thee the Tree
> Of Knowledge, knowledge both of good and evil;
> Forbids us then to taste, but his forbidding
> Commends thee more....
>
> (ix. 750-754)

In Kierkegaard's theory, the fall of man is his qualitative leap. "By the qualitative leap sin came into the world, and in this way it is continually coming into being."⁸ Before the "leap" is man's state of innocence. The relation between innocence, the feeling of guilt, and the fall, is explained by Kierkegaard as follows:

> Innocence is ignorance. In his innocence man is not determined as spirit but is soulishly determined in immediate unity with his natural condition. Spirit is dreaming in man. This view is in perfect accord with that of the Bible...(which refuses) to ascribe to man in the state of innocence a knowledge of the difference between good and evil....
> In this state there is peace and repose; but at the same time there is something different, which is not dissension and strife, for there is nothing to strive with. What is it then? Nothing. But what effect does nothing produce? It begets dread. Dreamingly the spirit projects its own reality, but this reality is nothing, but this nothing constantly sees innocence outside it.
> Dread is a qualification of the dreaming spirit, and as such it has its place in psychology. When awake, the difference between myself and my other is posited; sleeping, it is suspended; dreaming, it is a nothing vaguely hinted at.... The reality of the spirit constantly shows itself in a form which entices its possibility....
> One almost never sees the concept dread dealt with in psychology, and I must therefore call attention to the fact that it is something different from fear and similar concepts which refer to something definite, whereas dread is freedom's reality as possibility for possibility. One does not therefore find dread in the

⁷*Ibid.*
⁸*Ibid.*, p. 99.

least, precisely for the reason that by nature the beast is not qualified by spirit.... Dread is a sympathetic antipathy and an antipathetic sympathy".[9]

The fact that man is capable of experiencing dread is precisely his human quality.

In the state of innocence man is not merely an animal, for if at any time of his life he was merely an animal, he would never become a man. So then the spirit is present, but in a state of immediacy, a dreaming state.[10]

Innocence is a kind of ignorance, but not an animal brutality but an ignorance qualified by spirit, but which is precisely dread, because its ignorance is about nothing. Here there is no knowledge of good and evil, etc. But the whole reality of knowledge is projected in dread as the immense nothing of ignorance.... The prohibition alarms Adam (induces a state of dread) because the prohibition awakes in him the possibility of freedom.[11]

On the basis of this theory of Kierkegaard's we notice a correlation between Eve's dream in Book Four, and the events in Book Nine. We may not be able wholly to agree with William B. Hunter in that

It might be argued that the Fall took place before Book Nine in *Paradise Lost*, since in the dream inspired by Satan, Eve at least contemplated evil ways. Certain it is that the dream foreshadows the later event and to some degree at least motivates it.[12]

But the fact that the dream is the earliest anticipation of the fall cannot be overlooked. The dream is effective in so far as it is the earliest premonition of dread. Women are more prone to the presentiment of dread than men. Commenting on the Genesis Myth, Kierkegaard says:

Then follows the prohibition and the judgment. But the serpent

[9]*Ibid.*, pp. 37-8.
[10]*Ibid.*, p. 39.
[11]*Ibid.*, p. 40.
[12]*Milton on the Nature of Man*, pp. 14-15.

was more subtle than any beast of the field. He enticed woman
.... The myth represents as outward that which occurred inwardly.
What first we have to remark upon here is that woman is first seduced, and that thereupon she seduces man. . .dread is more natural to her than to man.[13]

The reason why woman feels more dread than man is not proof of any defect or inferiority in her. On the basis of the myth, it arises from the fact that she is created out of a precedent creature.

Eve is the derived being. True, she is created out of a precedent creature. True, she is innocent like Adam, but there is as it were a presentiment of a disposition, which indeed is not yet in existence, yet may seem like a hint of the sinfulness posited by reproduction. It is the fact of being derived which predisposes the individual....[14]

This passage goes a long way in explaining the connection between dream, dread, and the qualitative leap of the Original Sin through the fall. In creating the incident of the dream in Book Four and by relating its contents to the rest of the epic action, the subjective transformation which takes place in the Self of Eve, Milton shows a poetic insight into the true nature of human reality. *Paradise Lost* is an abiding monument to the timeless truths about human nature, perceived through the intuitions of both poetic and religious inspirations and translated into epic poetry through the medium of an all-inclusive myth.

To our first question, "What according to Milton is the nature of man?" the answer seems to be a dialectical one embracing the concepts of freedom, and the fall simultaneously. Man is that being who alone is capable of the fall. And what then is the fall? That which only man is capable of. The distinctive power of being able to transgress an imperative binding man to a state of "innocent identity" with nature, and through this transgression transcend this very condition of simplicity is the peculiarly human qualification. Etiologically speaking, it is determinative of the historical process itself. Using this radical conception, *Paradise Lost*

---

[13] *Op. cit.*, p. 42.
[14] *Ibid.*, pp. 42-3.

fuses myth and history into the synthesis of poetry. Whether the fall is paradoxically fortunate and unfortunate, or not, it begets the sympathetic antipathy, and the antipathetic sympathy, of dread. Milton's epic illustrates this psychological ambivalence of the fall even as it incorporates the theological ambivalence of simultaneous withdrawal through sin and the return to God through Grace.

In brief, we can only grasp Milton's concept of man in terms of the Biblical theocentric description of man as a being created in the image and likeness of God.

BIBLIOGRAPHY

ALLEN, D.C., *The Harmonious Vision*, Baltimore: The Johns Hopkins Press, 1954; enlarged edition, 1970.

AQUINAS, SAINT THOMAS, *Basic Writings of Saint Thomas Aquinas*, ed. and annotated, with an Introduction by Anton C. Pegis. New York: Random House, 1945, 2 Vols.

AUGUSTINE, ST., *On the Holy Trinity*, in Select Library of the Nicene and Post-Nicene, Fathers of the Christian Church, Vol. III, ed. by Philip Schaff, New York: Charles Scribner's Sons, 1917.

AUGUSTINE, ST., *Basic Writings of Saint Augustine*, edited, with an Introduction and Notes by Whitney J. Oates. New York: Random House, 1948, 2 Vols.

BAKER, HERSCHEL, *The Dignity of Man*, Cambridge: Harvard University Press, 1947.

BARKER, ARTHUR E., *Milton and the Puritan Dilemma*, Toronto: The University of Toronto Press, 1942. Reprinted 1964.

BARTH, KARL, *Church Dogmatics*, Vol. III; *Doctrine of Creation*, transl. by Knight, Harold and others, Edinburgh: T. & T. Clark, 1960.

BELL, MILLICENT, "Fallacy of the Fall in Paradise Lost," *PMLA*, LXVIII, 1953, pp. 863-83.

BROADBENT, J.B., *Some Graver Subject. An Essay on Paradise Lost*, London: Chatto & Windus, 1960.

BRUNNER, EMIL, *Man in Revolt; A Christian Anthropology*, transl. by Olive Wyon, Philadelphia: The Westminster Press, 1939.

BURNET, JOHN, "The Socratic Doctrine of the Human Soul," *Proceedings of the British Academy*, 1915-1916, London: Oxford University Press, Humphrey House.

BUSH, DOUGLAS, *Paradise Lost in Our Time. Some comments.* Ithaca, N.Y.: Cornell University Press, 1945; rpt. Gloucester, Mass.: Peter Smith, 1957.

CAIRNS, DAVID, *The Image of God in Man*, New York: Philosophical Library, 1953.

CALVIN, JOHN, *Institutes of the Christian Church*, Vols. I and II., ed. by John T. McNeil, tr. by Ford Lewis Battles. The Library of Christian Classics, Vol. XX, Philadelphia: The Westminster Press, 1960.

CASSIRER, ERNST, *An Essay on Man. An Introduction to the Philosophy of Human Culture*, New Haven: Yale University Press, 1944, 6th printing, 1951.

CASSIRER, ERNST, *The Logic of the Humanities*, tr. by Clarence Smith Howe, New Haven: Yale University Press, 1961.

CASSIRER, ERNST, *Philosophy and History. Essays presented to Ernst Cassirer*, ed. by Raymond Klibansky and H. J. Paton, Oxford: The Clarendon Press, 1936.

COPE, JACKSON I., *The Metaphoric Structure of Paradise Lost*, Baltimore: Johns Hopkins Press, 1962.

D'ARCY, M.C., *The Mind and Heart of Love. Lion and Unicorn. A Study in EROS and AGAPE*, London: Faber & Faber, second ed., rev., 1947.

DIEKHOFF, J.S., *Milton's Paradise Lost. Commentary on the argument*, London: Routledge and Kegan Paul, 1958, rpt. New York : Humanities Press, 1963.

HASTINGS, JAMES, ed., *Encyclopedia of Religion and Ethics*, viii (1955), pp. 641-8.

GREEN, CLARENCE C., "The Paradox of the Fall in Paradise Lost," *Modern Language Notes*, 1938 (liii), pp. 557-71.

GREENLAW, EDWIN, "A Better Teacher than Aquinas", *Studies in Philology*, XIV (April 1917), pp. 196-217.

GRIERSON, H.J.C., *Criticism and Creation*. Pennsylvania: The Folcroft Press, Inc. 1969 ; rpt. London: Chatto & Windus, 1949.

HUGHES, MERRITT Y., *John Milton. Complete Poems and Major Prose*, New York: The Odyssey Press, 1957.

HUNTER, WILLIAM B. JR., *Milton on the Nature of Man*. Folcroft, P.A.: The Folcroft Press, Inc., 1st publ., 1946; rpt. 1969.

The Interpreter's Dictionary of the Bible, New York: Abington Press, 1962.

HANFORD, JAMES HOLLY, *A Milton Handbook*, New York: Appleton-Century-Crofts, Inc., n.d., 4th ed.

KELLEY, MAURICE, *This Great Argument. A Study of Milton's De Doctrina Christina as a Gloss upon Paradise Lost*. Gloucester, Mass. : Peter Smith, 1962.

KERMODE, FRANK, *The Living Milton*, essays by various hands; collected and edited by Frank Kermode, London: Routledge and Kegan Paul, 4th impression, n.d.

KIERKEGAARD, SØREN, *The Concept of Dread*. A simple psychological deliberation oriented in the direction of the dogmatic problems of Original Sin, tr. by Walter Lowrie, Princeton: Princeton University Press, 1957.

LEWIS, C.S., *A Preface to Paradise Lost*, London: 1960; rpt., London: Oxford University Press, 1942.

LOVEJOY, ARTHUR O., "Milton and the Paradox of the Fortunate Fall", *ELH*, IV (1937), pp. 161-79.

LUTHER, MARTIN, *Luther's Works*, Vol. I. Lectures on Genesis, Chapters 1-5, tr. by George V. Schick, Saint-Louis : Concordia Publishing House, 1958.

MACCAFFREY, ISABEL GAMBLE, *Paradise Lost as "Myth"*, Cambridge, Mass.: Harvard University Press, 1959.

MAHOOD, M.M., *Poetry and Humanism*, New York: Kennikat Press, 1967.

MARILLA, E.L., *Milton and Modern Man, Selected Essays*, Alabama: University of Alabama Press, 1968.

NICOLSON, MARJORIE HOPE, *The Breaking of the Circle*, New York: Columbia University Press, 1960.

NIEBUHR, REINHOLD, *The Nature and Destiny of Man*, A Christian Interpretation, Gifford Lectures, New York: Charles Scribner's Sons, 1949.

PATTERSON, ALLEN, ed., *The Works of John Milton*. (18 v. in 21), New York: Columbia University Press, 1931-1938.

PETER, JOHN, *A Critique of Paradise Lost*, New York: Columbia University Press, 1960.

PLATO, *The Dialogues of Plato*, tr. by Benjamin Jowett. Oxford: Clarendon Press, 1953, 4th edition in 4 Vols.

RALEIGH, WALTER, *Milton*, London: Edward Arnold, 1905, second impression.

ROBINSON, H. WHEELER, *The Christian Doctrine of Man*, Edinburgh: T. and T. Clark, 1926, 3rd ed.

SAMUEL, IRENE, *Plato and Milton*, Ithaca, New York: Cornell University Press, 1947. rpt. 1965.

STEADMAN, JOHN M., *Milton's Epic Characters, Image and Idol*, Chapel Hill: The University of North Carolina Press, n.d.

STEIN, ARNOLD, *Answerable Style: Essays on Paradise Lost*, Minneapolis: The University of Minnesota Press, 1953.

STEWART, J.A., *The Myths of Plato*, Carbondale, Ill.: Southern Illinois University Press, 1960.

SVENDSEN, KESTER, *Milton and Science*, Cambridge: Harvard University Press, 1956.

TILLYARD, E.M.W., *The English Epic and its Background*, London: Chatto and Windus, 1954.

———, *Milton*, London: Chatto and Windus, 1946.

———, *Studies in Milton*, London: Chatto and Windus, 1964.

TOYNBEE, ARNOLD J., *A Study of History*, Vol. I, London: Humphrey Milford, Oxford University Press, 1935. 2nd ed.

WALDOCK, A.J.A., *Paradise Lost and its Critics*, Cambridge: Cambridge University Press, 1961.

WILLIAMS, ARNOLD, *The Common Expositor*, an account of the commentaries on Genesis, 1527-1633, Chapel Hill: The University of North Carolina Press 1948.

WOLFE, DON M., *Milton in the Puritan Revolution*, New York: Thomas Nelson & Sons, 1941; rpt. London: Cohen and West, 1963.

INDEX

INDEX

A Journal of English Literary History, 77n, 85n
ALLEN, D. C. *The Harmonious Vision*, 159
AQUINAS, ST. THOMAS, 5,30; *Summa*, 35n, 36, 36n, 40-41, 41n; *Basic Writings*, 159; On the image of God in man, 36
ARISTOTLE, *Poetics*, 93 ; on the plot, 93
AUGUSTINE, ST., 3, 5, 30, 40; on reason and rationality, 33 ; *Basic Writings*, 159 ; *On the Holy Trinity*, 33, 34-36, 34n, 35n, 159

BAKER, HERSCHEL, *The Dignity of Man*, 54, 159
BARKER, ARTHUR, *Milton and the Puritan Dilemma*, vii, 71n, 159
BARTH, KARL, 5, 28, 70, 74; *Church Dogmatics*, 6, 7, 70, 70n, 71n, 72-73, 74, 159; on creation, 71-74
BELL, MILLICENT, 87; "The Fallacy of the Fall in *Paradise Lost*", 88n, 159
BERGONZI, BERNARD, 13 ; "Criticism and the Milton Controversy", 14n
BROADBENT, J. B., *Some Graver Subject*, 152
BRUNNER, EMIL, 32; *Man in Revolt : A Christian Anthropology*, 31-32, 32n
BURNETT, JOHN, 20; "The Socratic Doctrine of the Human Soul", 20n, 159
BUSH, DOUGLAS, 8, 83 ; *Paradise Lost in our Time*, 83n, 159

CALVIN, JOHN, 5, 42, 54, 55; *Institutes of the Christian Religion*, 59, 59n, 159 ; on the dignity of man, 58-59 ; Calvin Theology, 62, 63
CAIRNS, DAVID, *The Image of God in Man*, 31n, 32n, 33n, 159
CASSIRER, ERNST, 91, 93, 94, 114; *An Essay on Man*, 91, 91n, 93, 94, 114, 114n, 159 ; *The Logic of Humanities*, 92, 92n, 93, 94, 159
Causality, the principle of, 9, 10
"Challenge-and-Response" theme, 106-117, 121
Civilization, the causes of genesis, 106-107
Chance, 39
COPE, JACKSON, I., *The Metaphoric Structure of Paradise Lost*, 16n, 159
Christian anthropology, 6; Christian dignity, 55-56; see also the DIGNITY OF MAN

DARCY, M.C., *The Mind and Art af Love*, 136n, 159
Devil's Challenge of God, 116
DIEKHOFF, J. S., 82; *Milton's Paradise Lost : A Commentary on the Argument*, 82n, 160
Dignity of Man, the conception of, 54-64
Divine-Demonic encounter, 115

ELIOT, T. S., 10
ELLMAN, RICHARD, 12
EMPEDOCLES, 102
Epic, the epic and the novel compared, 14-15; epic myth, 15
Epistles, Pauline, 31

Fall, 9, 61, 129, 150; the causes of, 129; the crisis of, 13, 148; Eve's fall, 140-143; the first step of, 143; the fall of man, discussed, 75-89, 153 ; Milton's treatment of the fall theme, 103, 137, 144; moral of the fall, 153; Fall as Original Sin, 157; "The Paradox of the Fortunate Fall", 86; the paradox of fall and freedom, 136-137; the psychological treatment, 153-154; the psychology of man and his fall, 76; fall as a qualitative leap, 155; fall story, 136; the technique of the treatment of fall, 9; the separate acts of transgression by Adam and Eve in the fall episode, 137; theories of fall, 81-89, 138; the theme of fall, 147

Faust, 102

Feeling-Quality in Adam's perception, 95

Freedom, the concept of, 39; freedom of man, 136; freedom and rationality, 40, 42

FRYE, NORTHROP, 8

Genesis, 3, 25, 28, 30, 45, 70, 97, 141; "Genesis Myth", 10, 97, 103, 137; and creation story, 137; and history, 100, 101-113

God, God the Son as the poetic realization of love, 125; God challenged through His creation, 121; God-Devil encounter, 118; God's image and likeness in man, 5, 7, 21, 32, 40, 66, 67, 127, 132-133, 150; the doctrine of God's image and likeness, 5-6; man's Godlikeness and the relationship between Adam and Eve, 66-67; personal relationship as an element in man's Godlikeness, 133-135

GREENLAW, EDWIN, 1, 4; "A Better Teacher than Aquinas", 100, 147

GREEN, CLARENCE, C., "The Paradox of the Fall in *Paradise Lost*", 77, 160

GRIERSON, HERBERT, T. C., *Criticism and Creation*, 83, 83n, 160; "Milton", 54, 54n

HANFORD, JAMES HOBLY, 1, 4, 7, 8; *A Milton Handbook*, 82n, 160

HASTINGS, JAMES, *Encyclopaedia of Religion and Ethics*, 160

Hate, as a theme in *Paradise Lost*, 95; see also the THEME OF LOVE

Hell, contrasted with the Garden of Eden, 127

HERAELITUS, Logos philosophy of, 35

History, and mythology, 96, 104; see also MYTH AND MYTHOLOGY

HUGHES, MERRITT, Y., *John Milton: Complete Poems and Major Prose*, viii, 38, 39n

HUNTER, WILLIAM B., 156; *Milton on the Nature of Man*, 156n, 160

IRENE, SAMUEL, 18; *Plato and Milton*, 19, 19n, 161

IRENAEUS, ST., 5, 28, 30

Image, divine, 6, 25, 62, 36, 158; see also GOD'S IMAGE AND LIKENESS IN MAN

Interpreter's Dictionary of the Bible, 160

Job, *The Book of Job*, 102, 103, 115

JOWETT, BENJAMIN, *The Dialogues of Plato*, 160

KELLEY, MAURICE, 11; *This Great Argument*, 160

KERMODE, FRANK, *The Living Milton*, 14n, 160

KIERKEGAARD, SØREN, 9, 136; treatment of fall and original sin, 154 *The Concept of Dread*, 9, 10, 10n, 154-155, 156-157, 160

LEAVIS, F. R., 8, 10, 82, 82n

LEWIS, C. S., 15, 82; *A Preface to Paradise Lost*, 34, 82n, 160

Love, Adam's idea of love, 139-140; love contrasted with hate, 144-145; love divine and human, 151; love the emotional principle of *Paradise Lost*, 95; the supremacy of love over evil, 106, 144; the theme of love, 135, 150, 151, 152

LOVEJOY, ARTHUR, O., "Milton and

the Paradox of the Fortunate Fall", 77, 85n, 86, 86n, 87, 160
LUTHER, MARTIN, 5, 42, 46, 47, 63; Luther's *Commentary on Genesis*, 43 43n, 44n, 46n, 47n, 50; Luther on man as God's image, 42-47; *Works*, 52, 52n, 53, 53n, 63, 63n, 160

MACCAFFREY, ISABEL, 97; *Paradise Lost as "Myth"*, 16n, 97n, 160
MAHOOD, M. M., *Poetry and Humanism*, 84, 84n, 160
MARILLA, E. L., *Milton and Modern Man*, 76, 76n, 85, 160
MASSON, DAVID, 96
Man, biblical theory of man, 66; the concept of man, 69; Christian doctrine of man, 29, 42; dignity of man, 18, 28, 30; man as the image of God (divine similitude), 34n, 42, 63, 88, 89, 126, 141
MILTON, on marriage, 67-69 ; on reason, 37-38
Works cited; *Areopagitica*, 37, 38; *Colasterion*, 67, 67n, *Considerations touching the likeliest means to remove Hirelings out of the church*, 56 56n, 58; *Doctrine and Discipline of Divorce* 61, 61n, 68; *De Doctrina Christiana* (also *Of the Christian Doctrine*), 11, 24, 26-27, 26n, 27-28, 28n, 38, 61-62, 96, 96n, 16, 117-118; *Paradise Lost*, 37-38, 39, 41, 48, 49-50, 51, 57-58, 60, 61, 63, 64, 66, 70, 86, 115, 117, 118, 120-130, 132-135, 138-140, 142-146, 150-155; *The Reason of Church-government Urg'd against Prelaty*, 55-56; *Tetrachordon*, 45-46, 55n, 58, 67
Modern Language Notes, 77n
Myth, mythology, 8, 9, 10, 13, 15; myth and plot distinguished, 9 ; mythology of *Paradise Lost*, 97; mythology and Genesis, 97; myth and history, 10, 90-100; mythic theory of the world, 94-95
Mutability, of Adam, 61

Necessity, 39
NICOLSON, MARJORIE HOPE, 96 ; *Science and Imagination*, 96, 160n; *The Breaking of the Circle*, 97, 160n
NIEBUHR, REINHOLD, *The Nature and Destiny of Man*, 160

Obedience, as a moral principle in *Paradise Lost*, 95
Orphism, 28

PATTERSON, ALLEN, *The Works of John Milton*, Columbia Edition, viii, 25n, 26n, 160n
PATTISON, MARK, 12
Pessimism in *Paradise Lost*, 86, 87
PETER, JOHN, *A Critique of Paradise Lost*, 160
PLATO, 11, 14, 18, 51; Platonic anthropology of alienation, 3, 22; Platonic doctrine of the human soul, 20; Plato's epistemology, 23; Platonic idealism, 2; Plato's philosophy, 48-50, 93; Platonism, 2, 4, 18, 28; the opposition of theoretical interest between Plato and Milton, 3, 18, 23
Works cited: *Phaedo*, 20-21, 21n; *Phaedrus*, 22, 22n; *Republic*, 21, 21n, 22, 22n, 49, 52; *Timaeus*, 49, 50, 52
Psalms, 30
Publications of the Modern Language Association of America, 88n

RALEIGH, SIR WALTER, i; *Milton*, 12, 160
Raphael's dialogues, 23-24; "scale-of-being" lecture, 49-52
Rationalism, Greek, 32
Rationality, as an element of God's image in man, 37; and freedom, 48; of man, 126
RAYMOND, KLIBANSKY, *Philosophy and History : Essays Presented to Ernst Cassirer*, 159
Reality, processive theory of, 9

Reason, 30; Christian definition of 36-37; as God's image in man, 32-33; the nature of 39; Right Reason, 77, 83
Reformation, 5, 29, 30, 54, 55
ROBINSON, H. WHEELER, *The Christian Doctrine of Man*, 161

Satan, as Hellish Hate, 126-127
Sin, Original, 25, 40, 42, 136
Soul, 18; Biblical view, 19, Greek theory of the soul, 19; Milton's view of the soul, 26-29
STEADMAN, JOHN M., *Milton's Epic Characters*, 93n, 161
STEIN, ARNOLD, Answerable Style, 84, 84n, 161
STEWART, J. A., *The Myths of Plato*, 16, 20, 20n, 161
Studies in Philosophy, 2, 4
SVENDSEN, KESTER, *Milton and Science*, 11, 161

Temporality, and mutability, 96
TILLYARD, E. M. W., 16, 18, 75; *The English Epic and its Background*, 16n; on the epic, 15-17; *Studies in Milton*, 80, 80n, 81, 86, 87, 87n, 161; Milton, 161
Time, in *Paradise Lost*, 96-97
Titanomachia, Greek myths of, 102
TOYNBEE, ARNOLD J., 10, 100, 102-113; on the Genesis myths, 101; on myths and modern fiction, 98-100; *A Study of History*, 97, 97n, 98n, 99, 99n, 102-108, 110-112, 121n, 161

Wager-motif, 108-113, 120-121
WALDOCK, A. J. A., 4, 8, 13, 77, 93; *Paradise Lost and its Critics*, 8, 13, 13n, 77, 78-79, 79n, 147-148, 148n, 149-150, 161; criticism of Waldock's theory, 98
Will, the nature of, 39
WILLIAMS, ARNOLD, *The Common Expositor*, 31-32, 31n, 32n, 161
WOLFE, M., *Milton in the Puritan Revolution*, vii, 161
WORDSWORTH, WILLIAM, 3

Yahweh, and Satan, 102; encounter between Yahweh and the Serpent, 137
Yin and Yang, 102

OHIO UNIVERSITY LIBRARY